Jerry Poteet's JEET KUNE DO SECRETS

VOLUME 2
ENERGY TRAINING

BY JERRY POTEET,
with FRAN JOSEPH

Disclaimer

Please note that the publisher and author of this instructional book are NOT RESPONSIBLE in any manner whatsoever for any injury that may occur by reading and/or following the instructions herein.

It is essential that before following any of the activities, physical or otherwise, herein described, the reader or readers should first consult his or her physician for advice on whether or not the reader or readers should embark on the physical activity described herein. Since the physical activities described herein may be too sophisticated in nature, it is essential that a physician be consulted.

c/o APG Media • P.O. Box 15159
N. Hollywood, CA 91615-9268
Tel: (866) 834-1249   Fax: (818) 487-4550
www.up-publications.com

ISBN: 0-86568-262-3
Library of Congress Control Number: 2006908081
© 2007 by Unique Publications. All rights reserved.
Published 2007. Printed in the United States of America.
Editor: Dave Cater
Designer: Suzanne K. Miller

To James
Jeet Kune Do brings us all into the light of understanding
Take care
Jerry Poteet

Jerry Poteet's Jeet Kune Do Secrets

Volume 2—Energy Training
By Jerry Poteet, with Fran Joseph

Table of Contents

Acknowledgments 5

Introduction 6

Behind Energy Training 7

Trapping 10

Basic Energy 22

Jeet Kune Do Energy Drills 23

JKD Trapping—Reference Point Training 52

Chi Sao 75

Conclusion 115

About the Author 116

BY JERRY POTEET, WITH FRAN JOSEPH

Acknowledgments

I would like to thank my students, Ed Monaghan, Octavio Quintero and Dimitri Therios, for their invaluable participation and contributions and editor Dave Cater, for giving me the opportunity to share my knowledge and experience.

I wish to thank my students all over the world for their support. I am most grateful to the readers of my Volume 1, who responded in so many kind ways directly to me. It is most encouraging and I welcome your comments on Volume 2 as well.

Finally, I cannot find the word to express my gratitude to my teacher, Bruce Lee. I only hope the readers will find the teacher, like I did, who will give them the insight they seek.

Introduction

Welcome to Volume 2 of my *Jeet Kune Do Secrets.* After hearing from so many readers who enjoyed my first book, I am confident that Volume 2 will help you to continue your search for the truth in Jeet Kune Do and martial arts.

This book explores what I refer to as "the missing link" in JKD—Bruce Lee's energy training. Although basic energy drills and applications were taught in the Los Angeles Chinatown class, the higher levels of this training were reserved for a select few at Bruce's house. Why did Bruce teach this way? First, energy training or *tactile awareness* training, must be done with a skilled partner, one on one. This training does not lend itself to group classes. Secondly, the system was so closely guarded, because the skills derived from this energy training are invaluable in combat. Unless you know you will always be twice as fast as and strong as your opponents, this training will help neutralize their superior physical attributes. Hopefully, you can appreciate why Bruce Lee and others before him kept this information and teaching method "close to the vest."

It is my goal to extend the awareness of today's remarkable martial artists, as was the case when my teacher did the same for me. He called his explanations a "finger pointing the way," and it is my wish to share this with everyone. If you are like me, you will discover that this energy training transcends the physical. Your awareness, and most importantly, your *self*-awareness, will increase to a level of profound understanding. And after all, isn't this the true, higher purpose of martial arts training?

BY JERRY POTEET, WITH FRAN JOSEPH

Behind Energy Training

Energy training! The very name conjures thoughts of mystical "chi" training or supernatural forces. Yet every martial art, and most professional contact sports for that matter, has some version of this training. Certainly, Greco-Roman wrestling employs a host of tactile awareness drills, as does Japanese jiu-jitsu, aikido, and of course, tai chi. Even American football players insist that some form of energy training is paramount to beating their opponent across the line. And for the martial artist, it is critical.

But first let's define "energy." In simple physical terms, energy is "pressure," and the ability to detect it or sense it. Once again, unless you know you will always much bigger and faster than all your opponents, you need to learn how to most efficiently *redirect energy.* How important are these skills? I have argued elsewhere that today's violent society makes these skills more critical that ever. Of course, mixed martial arts, grappling and boxing occur in this fighting range. But most importantly, so do most real-world, life-threatening encounters. (Think how difficult it would be to roll around between the seats or aisles of an airplane if terrorists try to take command. There is very little room to maneuver.) The fact is, most non-lethal fights begin with a shove, push or grab and usually precede to something much worse. The question that needs to be asked is, why is energy training neglected or missing in most martial arts curriculums?

Much of the emphasis on energy training was lost when big boxing gloves became popular with sparring. Using such large gloves eliminated many of the devastating weapons employed in this range. Even now, with "so-called" extreme fighting, these strikes are strictly prohibited. Another factor leading to the degeneration of energy training was the incorrect "trapping" that remains a favorite of many instructors. This version of trapping resembles more the child's game of patty-cake than true energy application. First, practitioners are slapping each other's arms down at the wrist instead of controlling the limbs and breaking the opponent's axis. Where are they controlling their opponents? Perhaps they just don't understand what it means to trap.

Incorrect Trapping Range

Dimitri attempts to trap too far away. Octavio's arms are not controlled **(1)**. When Octavio traps, he leaves Dimitri's arm free. There is no pressure against the body **(2)**.

1.

2.

Incorrect Control

Octavio tries to trap Dimitri without controlling both arms **(1)**. Dimitri clocks him with his free hand **(2)**.

1.

2.

Incorrect

Sometimes you can get lucky if you only control one arm **(1)**. But most of the time, you just get hit **(2)**.

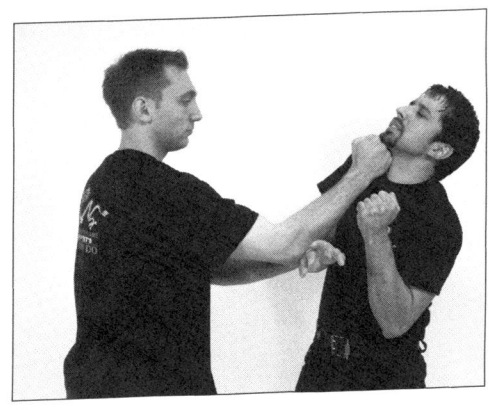
1.

2.

Correct

Octavio controls Dimitri with his elbow/body pressure, while he hits. Note that *both* arms are trapped and the centerline axis disrupted.

Trapping

This leads us to trapping, an exercise that is often discussed, but just as often misunderstood. Trapping is control, pure and simple. While virtually every martial arts system in existence has some form of trapping, it's very rare that these same systems share common techniques. All martial artists agree that trapping is necessary; what they disagree on is how best to make it happen. Whether the control comes in the form of holding or disrupting balance, trapping techniques are among the favorite attacks and counters of today's martial artist. Trapping occurs *inside* punching range; if you are busy pummeling your opponent's arms instead of attacking and controlling his axis (centerline), you are not really trapping no matter how fast you can wave your hands around or how flashy you look. My teacher, Bruce Lee, had a favorite expression: "To *feel* is to believe." And trust me, when you were on the receiving end of Bruce's trapping motion, you became a believer! I usually heard him say that just *after* he hit and controlled (trapped) me. I can attest to the utter helplessness of being thrashed, hit and knocked off balance in what seemed to be four different directions all at once. Shock waves literally exploded through my body. And there were also those times when Bruce did not even need to bother to hit. I witnessed him lap sao a person with so much force that the skeptic's head snapped back in a whiplash-like fashion. It was as though somebody had instantly removed all the bones the man's body.

This is the type of attack made famous through references in Sun Tzu's, *The Art of War*. If you are being hit and wrenched at the same time, you are fighting your balance as well as your opponent. Therefore, Jeet Kune Do trapping is a pristine example of the concept of "Divide and Conquer."

BY JERRY POTEET, WITH FRAN JOSEPH

Divide and Conquer

Jerry *pushes* into Ed with a punch, as he *pulls* with an arm control.

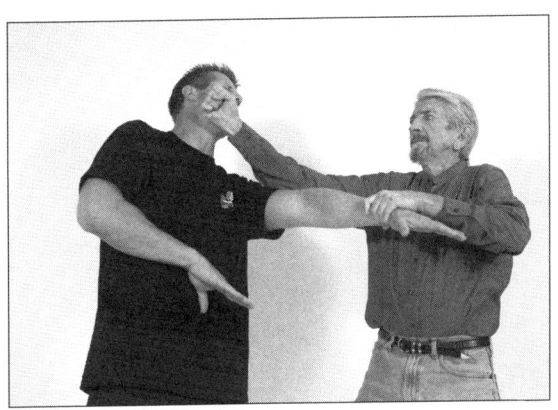

Even if you do not need to trap, you must *always* close the distance with some form of attack. Dimitri and Octavio square off **(1)**. Dimitri lands a low line kick **(2)**, then closes the gap with a hit **(3)**. Notice the leg trap.

1.

2.

3.

In my Jeet Kune Do curriculum, we train not only striking, hitting and kicking skills, but like professional athletes, we also develop awareness through several progressive drills. Bruce Lee was doing this long before anyone in sports ever heard about it. He realized that it was not enough to simply be faster and more powerful. Even with his amazing talent, he could not guarantee that everyone he squared off against was not going to be as fast or strong. Enter awareness drills and training; tactile awareness, in particular, can cut another person's speed in half. "How is that possible?" you ask.

Consider this: Four things must occur for you to stop an attack.
1. See or visually detect the attack
2. Interpret or figure out the nature of the attack (e.g., a hook, a kick, etc.)
3. Decide how to respond
4. Counter the attack

Octavio sees Dimitri enter hitting range **(1)** and launches a straight lead **(2)**. Dimitri slips the punch and shoots in on Octavio **(3)**.

1.

2.

3.

Now you see why Bruce used to say, "To *see* is to be deceived." Visually interpreting an attack is much too slow when the attack is at close range—which it almost always is. When things are fast and furious, there is not sufficient time to go through all the above steps. Even if you are equally matched in speed, your opponent has already initiated the attack. You are already *at least two beats behind* and playing "catch up."

If, on the other hand, you have cultivated your tactile awareness through energy training and "listened with the arms," as Bruce used to say, you do not have to rely on eyesight. Instead, you simply "respond like an echo" and turn your adversary's attack against him in a split second. When no conscious deliberation or thought interfers with your movement, "IT" hits. And then you are truly on your way to attaining higher levels of martial arts.

This time, when Dimitri slips Octavio's punch **(1)**, Octavio stays attached (maintains contact) and hits with a trap **(2)**. No need to look once contact is made! "Stay with what comes…

1.

2.

Martial artists are always claiming, "Trapping doesn't work." And in their particular case, they are right! It won't work for them, because their skill level is so low. I have watched students slap each other's arms for five or six moves before someone finally throws a punch, instead of controlling and hitting and ending the fight in a few explosive moves. I have even observed people "trapping" one of the opponent's arms, while the other dangles free at his side. Why is his opponent cooperating? He can retaliate at any time, and render his attacker's "trapping" useless. Is it any wonder trapping "doesn't work" for them! Finally, to make up for lost knowledge many martial artists simply add a hasty pak sao (slapping hand) to an arm and rush right into grappling. If you're sure that you're a better grappler than your opponent or if you have the luxury of facing only one opponent, this approach might work. And then again, it might not. Why take the risk? If you lose an entire arsenal of weapons and a complete fighting range, you will be doomed to grapple, whether or not you want it. A skilled martial artist controls the range, tempo and outcome of a fight. (By the way, energy training is just as useful on the ground as it is standing, but the choice should be yours.)

Three Controls of Trapping

Dimitri and Octavio face off **(1)**. Dimitri intercepts Octavio's punch with an eye jab **(2)**. *Control the tempo (time)*. Dimitri traps (controls) and slices to the throat **(3)**. *Control the space (distance)*. He finishes with trap/hit and smother **(4)**. *Control the centerline (axis)*. Trapping is used only when you are unable to hit or strike.

1.

2.

3.

4.

BY JERRY POTEET, WITH FRAN JOSEPH

As my teacher used to constantly emphasize, "Always think of hitting!" The trap is a by-product of hitting. Unless you are trying to hit, trapping will not work because it is not necessary. Hit if you can hit successfully without your attack being obstructed. When applying energy training in actual combat, the first JKD Dictum is universal: **Always Hit First!**

If you can hit, just hit! No matter what the combat range, the first movement should be aggressive, not defensive. Before an opponent can hit, tackle or choke you, he has to get past your longer-range kicks, strikes and punches. Next, he has to survive your closer range elbows, hits, forearm smashes, shoulder strikes and even headbutts. But if he manages to get through your barrage, you will be very grateful indeed for the skill that comes with JKD energy training!

My teacher emphasized energy training for another important reason: to make the martial artist perfectly comfortable at a very close range of combat. Where most martial arts stop or resort to leaving their feet, we really kick it into gear. Jeet Kune Do energy training helps the martial artist feel his opponent's intentions. You learn to flow or fit in with his force, effortlessly using (borrowing) his strength, force, speed and pressure (energy) against him. Usually happening inside punching range, it can be used not only against punches and wild haymakers, but also against locks, tackles, grappling and wrestling attacks.

Bruce Lee said his teacher, Yip Man, did not even have to use punches. Instead, most of the time, he simply utilized what we now call "traps" to neutralize and control much bigger opponents. Bruce told me how Yip Man controlled him at this range, even though at the time the wing chun grandmaster was old and frail. My instructor was sufficiently impressed, if not awed, by this skill. He exclaimed, "Jerry, I couldn't get in on him!" I questioned him about this and asked, "You mean from Chi Sao Range?" He replied, "No, every range." How is this possible? He said that Yip Man possessed incredible *perception* and *awareness* of any gesture, no matter how slight, in every range of combat. After hearing the story, I saw the emphasis on energy training much more so than before in our workouts. It was as if we were guinea pigs Bruce was using in an experiment. To me, he was already untouchable. But after he dedicated himself to cultivating his perceptual and tactile awareness, he became almost superhuman!

Control at First Contact!

Dimitri and Octavio face each other **(1)**. When Dimitri tries to slap away Octavio's front guard, Octavio does not resist **(2)**. Instead of pulling his arm back, Octavio stays connected and hits with a forearm trap **(3)**. Then he flows to a hook **(4)** when he feels "emptiness" (no resistance).

1.

2.

3.

4.

By now you are seeing that energy training or sensitivity training does not only help in close quarters, but serves just as well from a non-contact point of view. Although it starts in close range, energy training eventually heightens your awareness in all ranges of combat. First, you rely on your opponent's movements to redirect and control his force. You eventually extend your awareness ("extend your chi") and free yourself of even having an opponent. The mind, body and spirit flow together without the distraction of acknowledging your opponent, and "**IT**" hits. This is the kind of true liberation, Zen swordsmen, tai chi masters and Shaolin Monks strived to achieve. And from experiencing first-hand the "Young Master," I know it is possible for all of us. We have only to begin…

Before you can attain a high skill level in any endeavor, you have to start with a foundation. For Bruce, the energy training started with what he called "energy drills," which he took from chi sao. He felt that without the fundamental understanding of energy drills, trapping was merely a pre-arranged sequence and therefore, useless. You just can't jump into trapping or chi sao without these drills. One had to be built on a solid foundation of the other. Once the energy drills are second nature, every contact, no matter what range, becomes a reference point. You simply learn the trapping in arm range, then graduate to use it at any range—standing or ground—where tactile contact is possible. Unlike drills, trapping hands is a much more active way of learning energy training.

Consider this: Even under extreme conditions of force and speed, football players must develop an awareness of the ball and opponent. In the same way, high-stage trapping calls on second-nature responses. There is no time for conscious deliberation when anything goes and attacks and counters are no longer pre-arranged. Practitioners often make the mistake of remaining in "trapping mode," or use their skills against another partner performing a similar technique. To become battle-tested, you must train trapping against all kinds of attacks and in all ranges of combat. Otherwise, you will remain forever in the first stage of reference points. This is the stage where people become slap-happy and repeat set sequences ad nauseam. The Internet is rampant with videos of students doing what I call "psychic martial arts;" that is, if you do this, I counter with that, etc. But what if he doesn't do what you expected? You have only attained skill level in this area when you can respond to anything an opponent throws at you. It bears repeating that the trapping hands are only energy drills and constitute one very necessary step toward instilling and maintaining tactile awareness. However, they do not constitute the end of energy training.

The highest stage of energy training in Jeet Kune Do is Chi Sao or energy hands. Anyone who thinks this type of training is not important in martial arts should watch police videos or bar fights. Unarmed combat lives here. I had a particularly difficult time adjusting to this range, since before I trained with Bruce Lee I was a kicker with an extensive karate background.

I have been blessed with long legs, so it was fairly easy for me to remain in long range and kick. It was easy, that is, until I met Bruce Lee! And if that wasn't bad enough, another member of our group, Daniel Lee, got inside my kicks and used his Olympic-level boxing on me. Clearly, I needed more close-range fighting tools along with the uppercuts and hooks I'd already learned. Chi sao became my savior.

Let's summarize: The progression in Jeet Kune Do energy training is:
1: Energy drills; 2: Trapping; 3. Chi Sao.

Before we begin with the energy drills, let's look at how Bruce Lee broke down all the possible combat positions in hand range. He showed me every possible position for fighting on the wooden dummy, insisting they were the only possible options, "unless someone grew another arm." Let's take a look.

Two Hands Outside—Right.

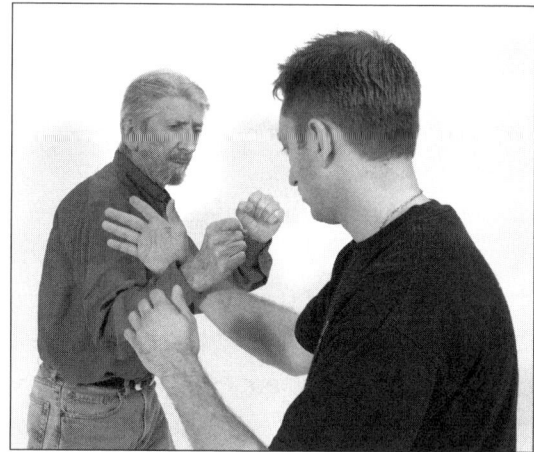
One Hand Inside and One Hand Outside.

Both Hands Inside.

One Hand Inside and One Hand Outside.

Two Hands outside to My Right.

Two Hands Wide.

What we call Reference Point Trapping in JKD begins with both hands outside, since we blade the body into a lead. In traditional Wing Chun or Wing Tsun, practitioners' bodies are square to the opponent, so all positions apply from the first reference point.

Energy Drills in Jeet Kune Do frequently start with one person having both hands outside, while his partner has both hands inside. All these positions cover every conceivable arms' position you can find himself in with an opponent. Here are a few common combat scenarios.

(1) Common boxing or trapping set-up. Both people have two arms outside. **(2)** Common clinch set-up. Both have one arm inside and one arm outside. **(3)** Dimitri attempts a waist grab with both arms inside. **(4)** Trap and hit with one hand inside and one outside.

1.

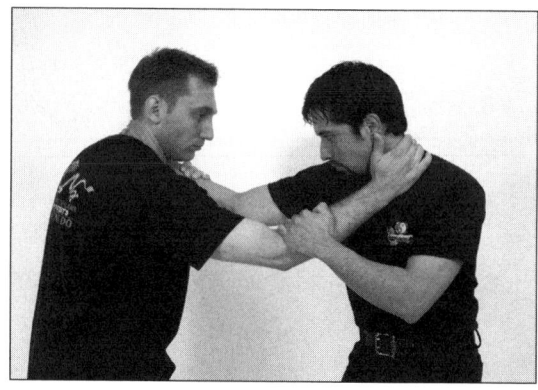

2.

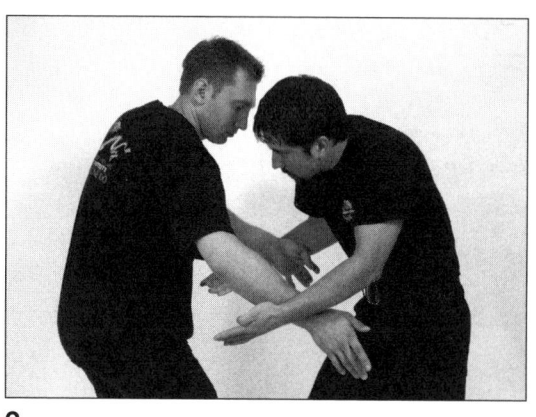

3.

4.

(5) Both have two arms outside. **(6)** Choke and grab with both arms inside. **(7)** Trap/hit with both hands outside. **(8)** Jerry stops a neck grab by hitting inside with two hands.

5.

6.

7.

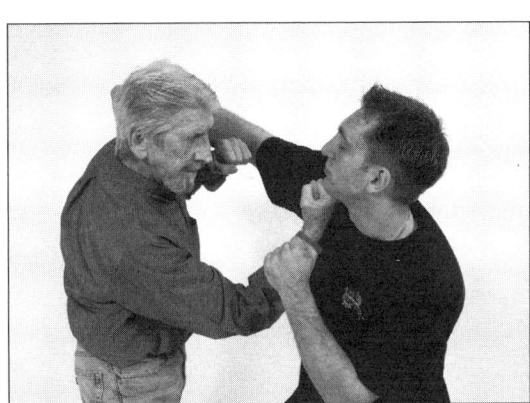

8.

From the pictures, you can clearly see that only Chi Sao covers all positions. From my years of teaching I have learned it is best to describe the Chi Sao position as a sphere. In my JKD training, we refer to attacks from any of these positions as "Cutting the Sphere." From the top, you would see that it is 360 degrees by 360 degrees. Instead of resembling a ball, Chi is **Pi** with its four axis. You not only can go left to right, but also backward and forward.

The Sphere contains:
    Diagonal
    Vertical
    Horizontal

Now that we understand *why* we do energy training and *how*, or what progression we use, we are ready for the *what* or particular skills. These are the Jeet Kune Do Energy Drills.

Basic Energy

As noted previously, the first function of these drills is to *control* your opponent at a close range, and then every range.

After many years of practice and teaching I have found the truth in the four energies: *forward, springing, dissolving and sticking.*

- **Forward Energy**—This is the fundamental principle of always moving TOWARD YOUR OPPONENT. When he backs up or sidesteps, you stay on him with your attack. Although this might seem obvious, you can watch any martial arts or boxing contest on television, and notice that the combatants do not apply this principle. Instead, they throw a combination and back up. Then their opponent does the same, and on and on. Why give the opponent another chance? When your strikes are blocked or countered, merely use the energy to redirect your attack and continue with unrelenting forward energy.

- **Sticking**—Sticking is a combination of the other three energies. When you stick, you stay attached to your opponent. When he pulls back, you not only move forward, but remain attached and maintain contact. Some people prefer to keep tremendous forward pressure on the opponent. But Bruce Lee was different; when he performed this technique, he had such sensitivity you did not even feel that he was making contact until it was too late.

- **Springing Energy**—Taking advantage of any opening, no matter how small or temporary. Spring through the gap with your attack and strike like a cobra! When you can work on an intuitive level and have internalized the principles, this is already a part of you. Then, you "respond like a shadow."

- **Dissolving Energy**—Used to neutralize a stronger force or attack. To dissolve an attack, you *redirect* or intercept an opponent's force. Bruce Lee called this, "feeling the opponent's *intentions*" and using them against him.

All four energies are taught in the Energy Drills.

BY JERRY POTEET, WITH FRAN JOSEPH

Jeet Kune Do Energy Drills

The first step in Jeet Kune Do energy training involves *energy drills*. These are your building blocks and constitute the support for all chi sao, trapping and combat applications. Originally adapting them from Wing Chun, Bruce Lee later modified the movements to suit Jeet Kune Do's principles and ready stance. Many of the modifications were structural in nature, since JKD blades the body into a lead, with only one side forward. Therefore, it is imperative to do them in proper order. First comes Cross Energy Drill. It is the most basic and the one you'll most often turn to in times of combat.

Cross Energy Drill—Outside Your Arm—Unmatched

In this drill, your partner is square while you hold out your punch in a lead. He must block your punch across his body. Remember, these are tactile training drills, not actual fighting. But Bruce could move your body and arms into these positions at will!

Dimitri blocks Jerry's punch **(1)** across his own body (past center). Jerry rolls with the force or energy of the block and stays attached **(2)**. He then borrows the energy of the block to fire a backlist **(3)**.

Many people try to speed this drill up by grabbing too soon. They flail their arms in a circular motion, trying to look fast. You have to wait for pressure or energy; otherwise you are missing the point of the drill.

1.

2.

3.

Incorrect

When Jerry parries across his body **(1)**, Dimitri grabs Jerry's arm too soon **(2)**. Sensing the lack of pressure, Jerry grabs both hands (trap) and hits **(3)**.

1.

2.

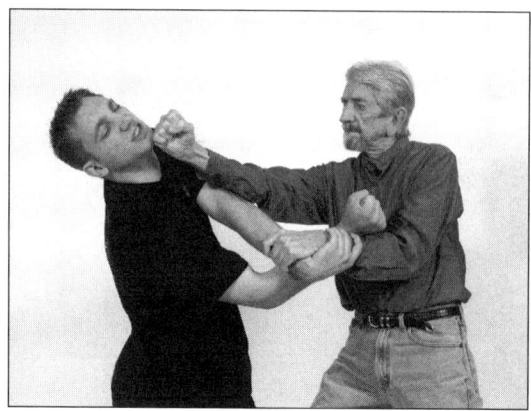

3.

Incorrect

Dimitri responds to Jerry's Cross Energy **(1)**. He slaps the arm down and retracts his fist **(2)**. Jerry feels the lack of pressure and hits in the gap **(3).**

1.

2.

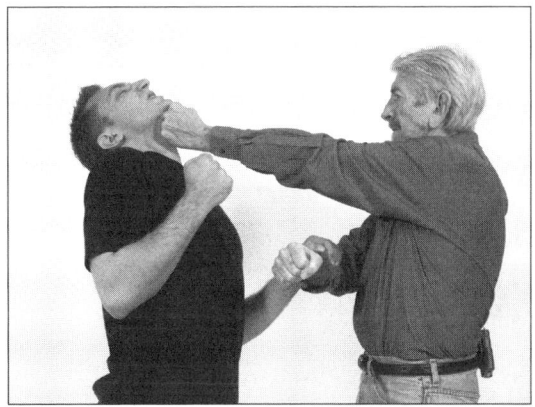

3.

Incorrect

If the grab is too high **(1)**, Jerry hits in the gap **(2)**.

1.

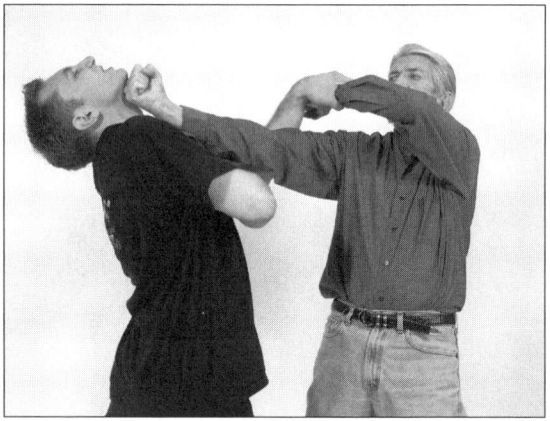

2.

Incorrect

Ed blocks Jerry's punch too far down at the wrist **(1)**. Jerry hits through the gap **(2)**. Jerry shoots a punch through the gap **(3)**.

1.

2.

3.

This drill's progression is to feed your partner energy across the body, then the shoulder and finally the head. All the energy drills have three stages, but for the purposes of this book, we will remain on the first. Remember, we are always attacking the axis, or centerline. Your pressure should always be there and not to the sides.

Common Application:

Ed uses a shoulder roll against a rear cross.

Cross Energy Drill *Inside* Arm

As before, hold your punch out in a lead; your partner is facing you square **(1)**. This time, he blocks *inside* your arm **(2)**. Sandwich his arm (trap) and continue his energy with your own hit **(3)**.

1.

2.

3.

Ed parries Jerry's punch across and inside Jerry's arm **(1)**. Jerry remains attached and rolls with the blocking energy **(2)**. Jerry controls (traps) with a hit **(3)**.

1.

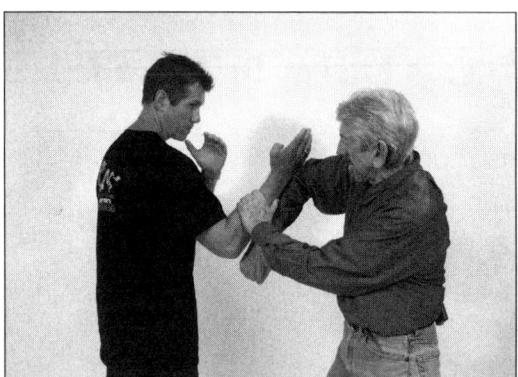

2.

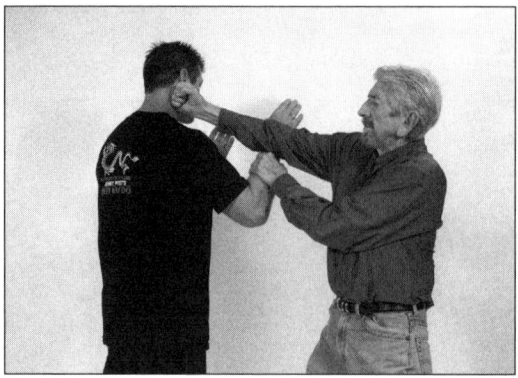

3.

Incorrect

Jerry parries Ed's punch inside and across his arm **(1)**. Ed pulls back and loses contact with Jerry's arm **(2)**. Since there is no trap with the elbow, Jerry is free to hit **(3)**.

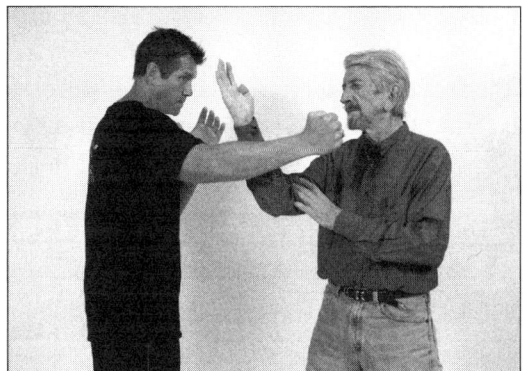
1.

2.

3.

This sequence demonstrates that if you do not punch at axis, you lose economy. If he grabs down and pistons the arm back he loses momentum and has to re-start his energy. Why lose a beat of time?

Harmonious Spring

This drill trains you to hit when pressure is released. The arms should automatically spring forward. It also teaches the detection of fine motions. If you can feel the soft cupping and closing of the hands, then gross motions will be no problem.

Both Ed and Jerry are square to each other **(1)**. The person with both hands on the outside jut sao's and punches **(2)**. The person with both hands on the inside sticks and *springs forward* with a punch **(3)**. Once you are comfortable, do this drill with your eyes closed.

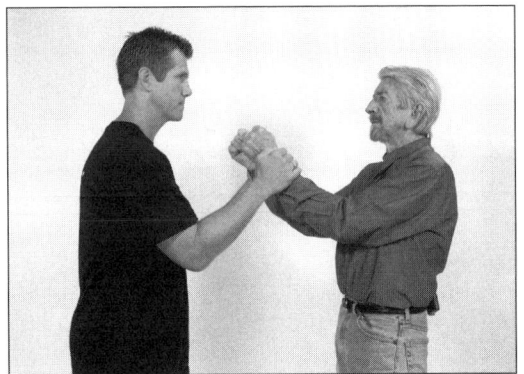

1.

2.

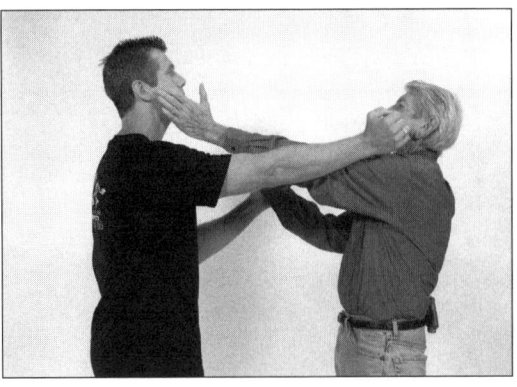

3.

Incorrect

Ed bends his wrists on the outside of Jerry's arms in a classical fook sao position **(1)**. Jerry traps his arm against his body and breaks the wrist **(2)**.

1.

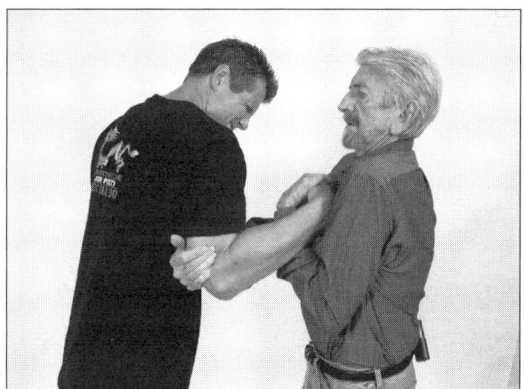

2.

Classical Answers

This drill was traditionally practiced with Tan Sao and Boang Sao responses, instead of the hit. Ed and Octavio prepare to perform the harmonious spring drill **(1)**. Ed pulls down on Octavio's arms **(2)**. When Ed releases and punches, Octavio responds with Boang Sao **(3)**. When he punches again, Octavio responds with Tan Sao **(4)**.

1.

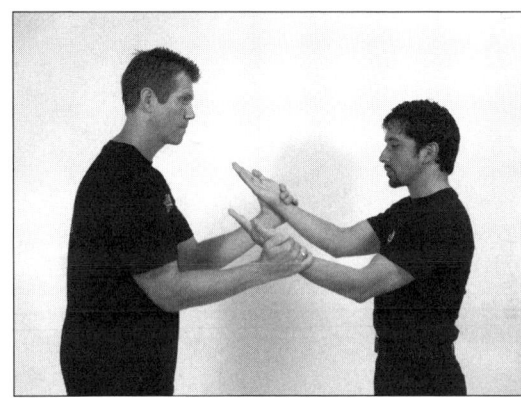

2.

3.

4.

BY JERRY POTEET, WITH FRAN JOSEPH

The JKD Way—No Passive Moves

Both violate the No Passive Moves (NPM) principle of Jeet Kune Do! Answer with a hit instead of a block. This time when Ed pulls down **(1)**, Jerry responds with a hit when Ed tries to punch **(2)**. The hit is always the correct answer!

1.

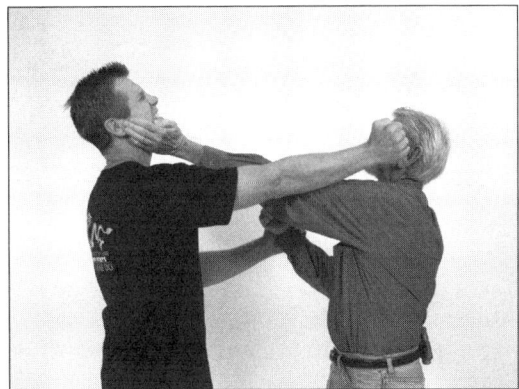

2.

The three stages to this drill are: Jut Sao, where you pull softly and hit **(1).** Turn Loose, where you simply turn loose and hit **(2)** and disengage, where you exhibit a complete lack of pressure **(3)**. This is what Bruce Lee called "emptiness." This drill teaches you to respond with an instantaneous slap to a lack of pressure or a release of pressure. In the final stage of this drill, you can mix the three previous stages.

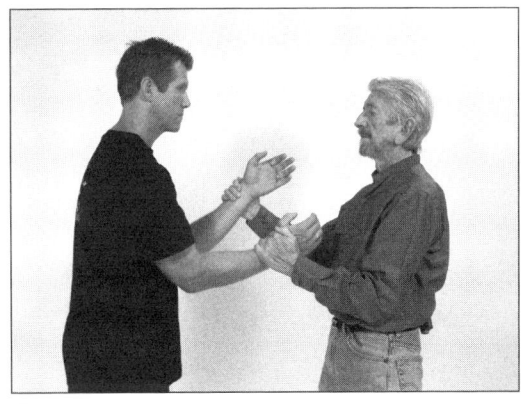

1.

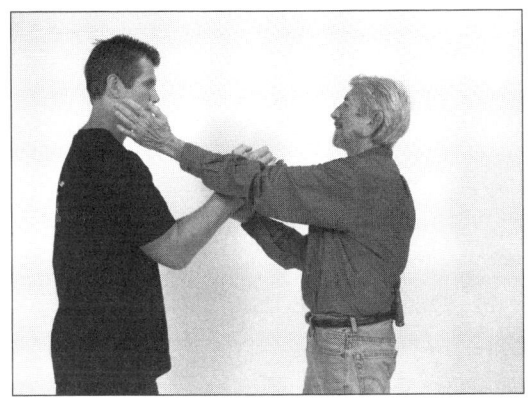

2.

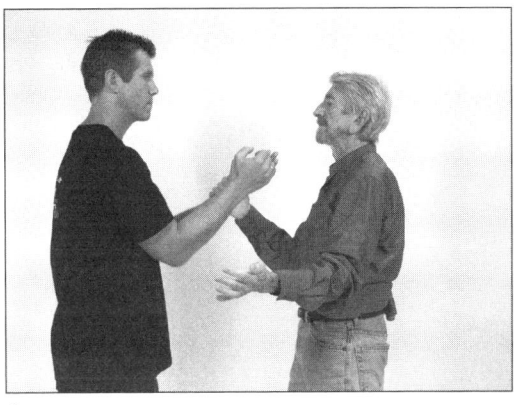

3.

| 33

Waum (Cross) Pak Drill

This drill teaches coordination in both hands; as one hand follows energy back, the other moves forward to hit. Square to each other, Jerry punches Ed **(1)**. Ed cross-paks and rolls the arm under to control and hit **(2)**. Your punch should cover his nose **(3)**.

1.

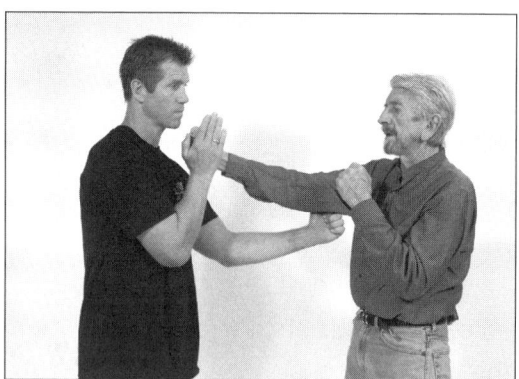

2.

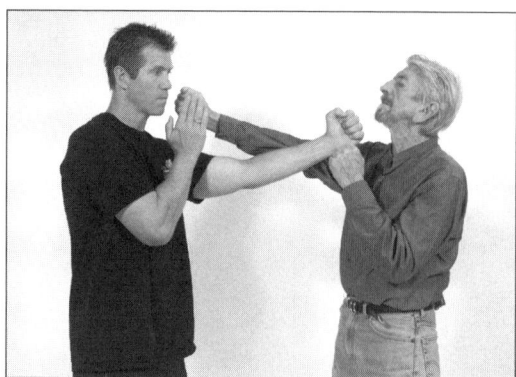

3.

Incorrect

When Ed punches Octavio **(1)**, he retracts his arm while parrying **(2)**. Keep a tight structure **(3)**.

1.

2.

3.

Progression

The Harmonious Spring Drill and Waum Pak go together. At the next stage, you can mix in Lap Sap Switch Drill.

Boang Sao Drill

This essential drill teaches you how to dissolve greater force and return with your own. It is also the quickest way to cover or protect your center. Very similar to a boxer's shoulder roll, it is used frequently in the bladed body JKD structure.

Ed and Jerry face each other in unmatched leads **(1)**. Ed throws a strong punch **(2)**. Jerry deflects by raising his elbow higher than his wrist **(3)**. He rolls to a backfist hit and trap **(4)**. You have to dissolve the energy by lifting my elbow and deflecting the strike while hitting. This is *not* a block.

1.

2.

3.

4.

Incorrect

Ed Boang Sao's Dimitri's punch and rolls to a backfist **(1)**. Instead of waiting for the pressure, Dimitri reaches for the punch **(2)**. Ed traps both hands and hits **(3)**.

1.

2.

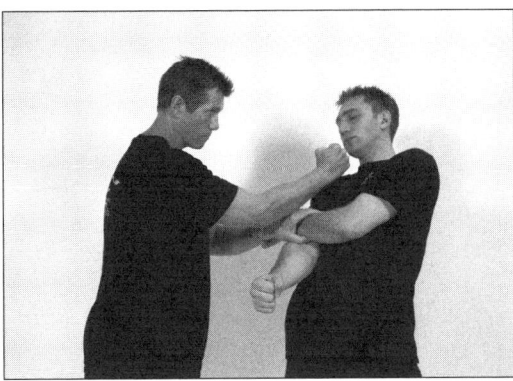

3.

As with the Cross Energy drill, if you reach out to catch the punch and speed up the drill, you resemble children playing patty-cake. Start at a slow speed to recognize tactile pressure. Remember: to *feel* is to believe!

Incorrect

Many people beat up the arms, rather than the head. Why waste energy on hitting something that will not stop a fight? Ed Boang Sao's Dimitri's punch **(1)** and punches at his wrist **(2)**. Dimitri fires a fingerjab with his free arm **(3)**.

1.

2.

3.

Incorrect

If you do not stay attached there is no control and subsequently, no trap. Don't rush it! This is *not* a backfist drill or a lap sao drill. When contact is made at the wrist, the elbow should already be up **(1-3)**.

1.

2.

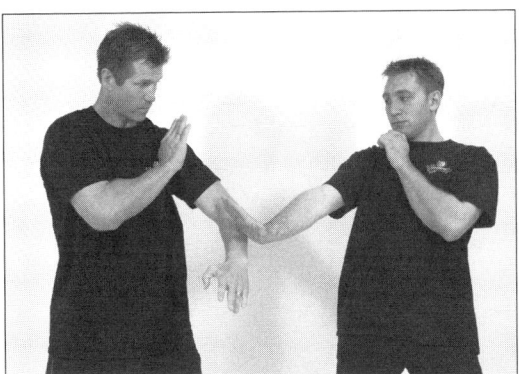

3.

First Progression

When Ed delivers a strong pull and hit **(1)**, Jerry goes **(2)** with the energy ("give way"), switches leads and hits **(3)**.

1.

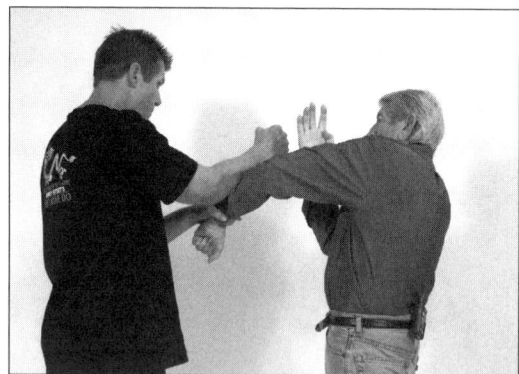

2.

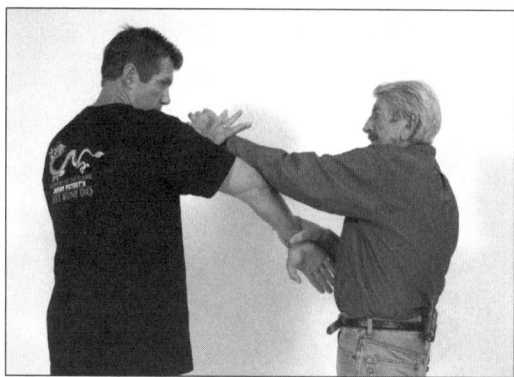

3.

Second Progression

Stick and stay attached. When they pull **(1)**, Jerry follows the arm in and hits low **(2)**.

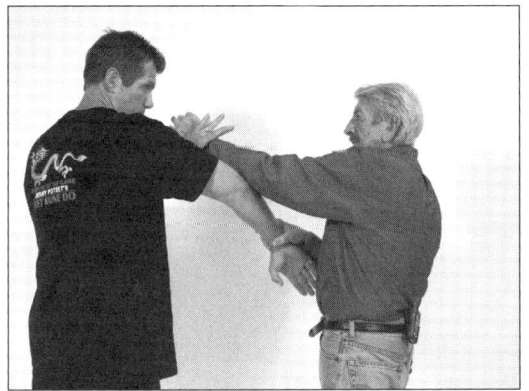
1.

2.

Third Progression

Use the NPM Principle to hit on every move! Jerry inserts a left-hand hit **(1)**, then finishes with a right backfist and trap **(2)**.

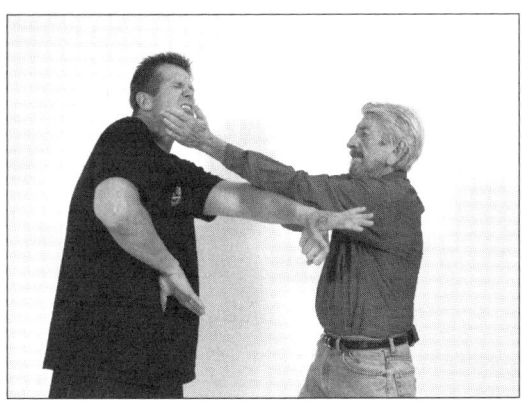
1.

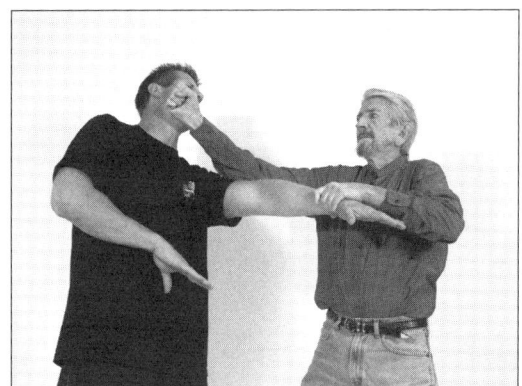
2.

You can add an element of broken rhythm training here by inserting a riposte. When Jerry hits low, Ed counters with a tan sao **(1)**. Jerry goes to "The Open Side" with an elbow smash **(2)** and lock (trap).

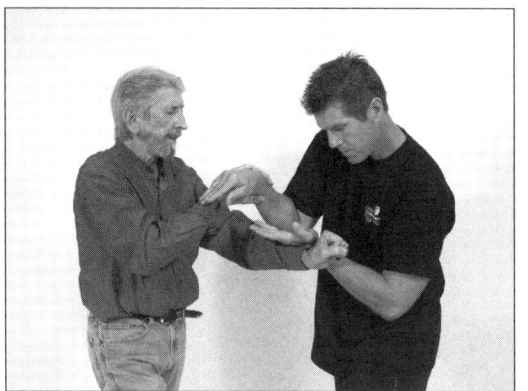
1.

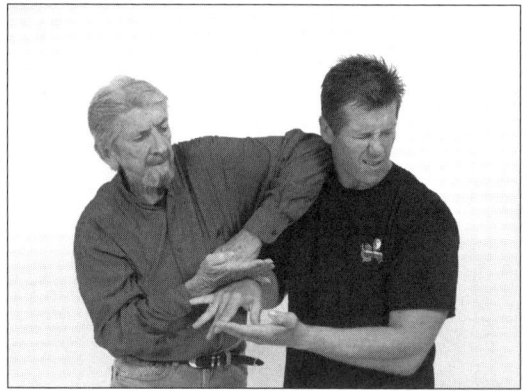
2.

Applications:

Dimitri grabs Ed's wrist and pulls **(1)**. Instead of resisting, Ed borrows the pulling energy to the elbow **(2)**.

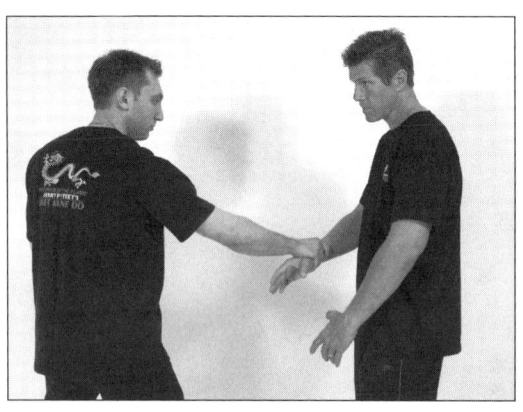
1.

2.

Dimitri throws a rear cross and Ed shoulder rolls **(1)**. Ed rolls out to counterpunch **(2)**.

1.

2.

Inside Lap Sap Switch Drill

This drill teaches you to flow with energy and recover the center. It is especially useful for grabs and clinches. Dimitri and Jerry start square in classical position **(1)**. When Dimitri pulls with a lap sao **(2)**, Jerry turns at the waist **(3)** and punches at Dimitri's center **(4)**.

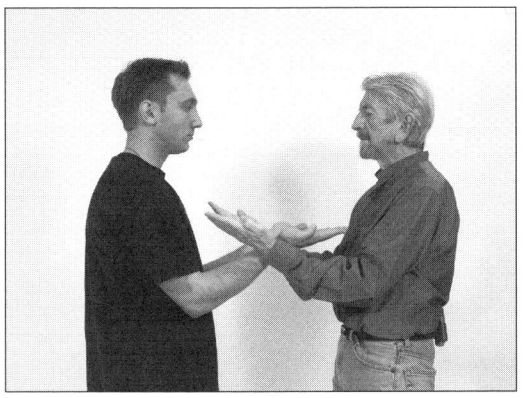
1.

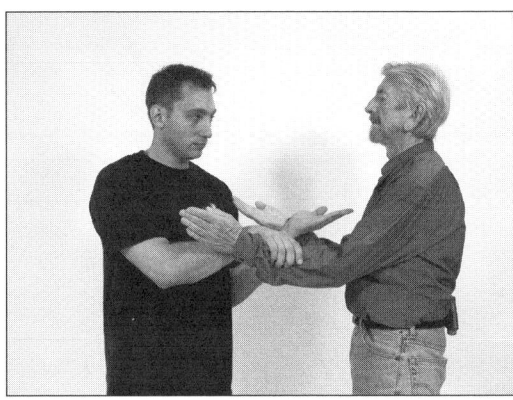
2.

3.

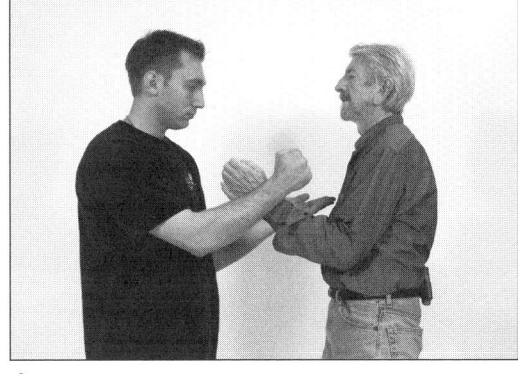
4.

Make sure you extend the arm and go with the pull; don't resist! Remember, you are always fighting for the center. Don't let your punch drift to the sides.

Incorrect

Octavio lap sao's with his elbow up, instead of turning at the waist **(1)**. Dimitri switches inside **(2)** and hits him in the gap **(3)**.

1.

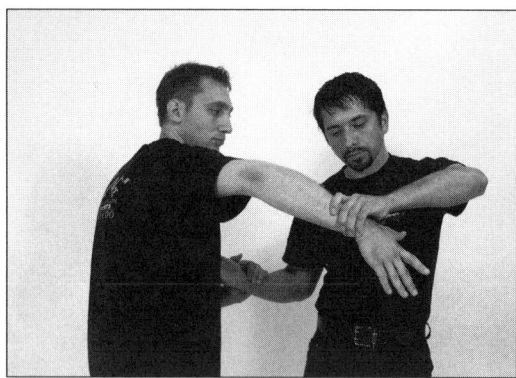

2.

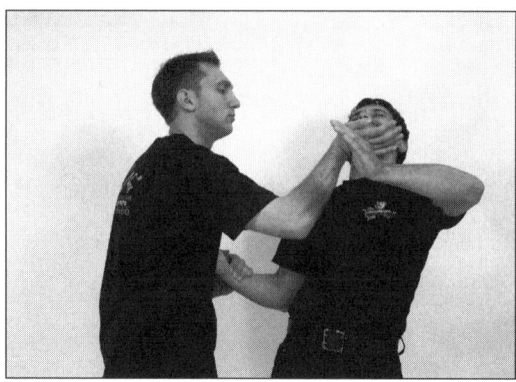

3.

Jerry and Dimitri face off **(1)**. Jerry pulls and Dimitri switches inside **(2)**. Jerry elbows instead of hitting **(3)**.

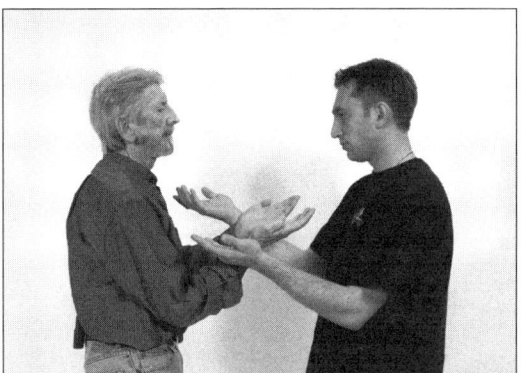

1.

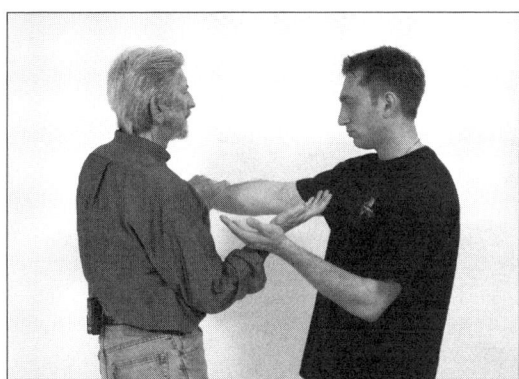

2.

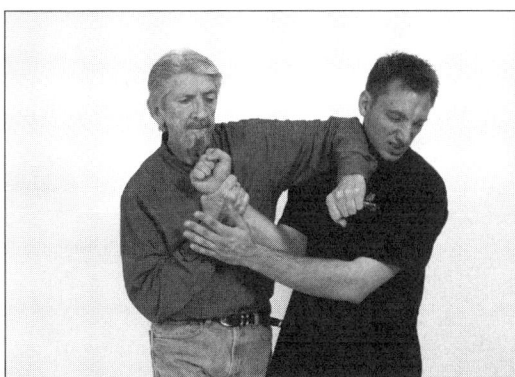

3.

You can smother the inside switch drill. Dimitri and Jerry begin the Inside Switch Drill **(1)**. When he switches inside I drop my elbow to hit **(2)**. If he counters with a Boang Sao, I follow it up to a slice to the throat **(3)**.

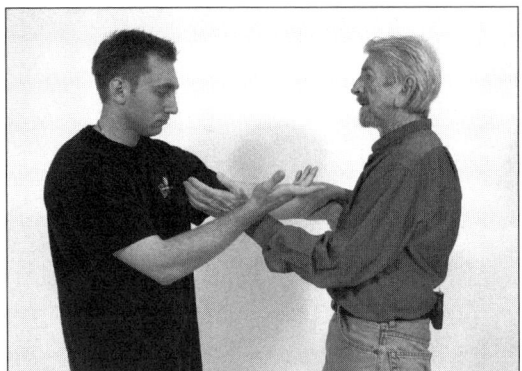

1.

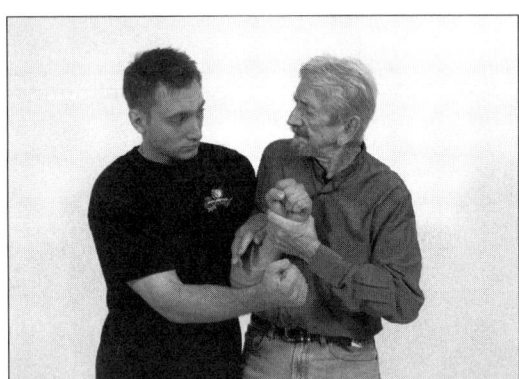

2.

3.

BY JERRY POTEET, WITH FRAN JOSEPH

Wrist Elbow Principle

This is one of the most useful principles in Jeet Kune Do energy training. It is very simple: when there is pressure at the wrist, the elbow comes up. When there is pressure at the elbow, the wrist comes up. Obvious applications are against grabs, locks, etc.

Switch Drill Applications:

Dimitri faces Octavio **(1)**. Dimitri fires a punch **(2)**. He prepares to Lap Sao and hit **(3)**. Octavio switches inside **(4)** and hits with a trap **(5)**.

1.

2.

3.

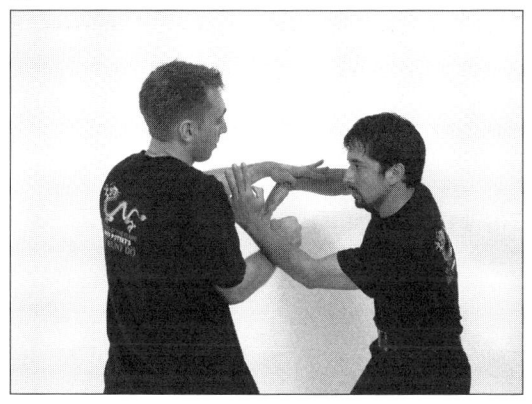
4.

5.

Application from a Clinch:

Ed and Dimitri tie up **(1)**. Dimitri switches inside **(2)**. He continues the switch to a palm smash **(3)**.

1.

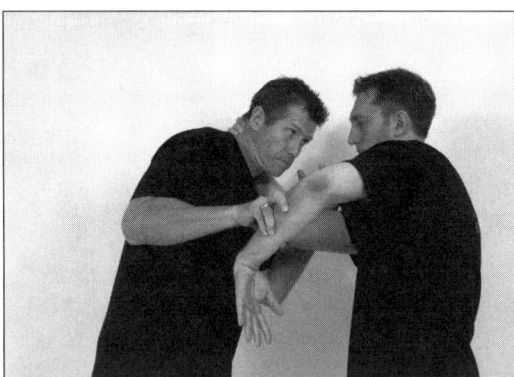

2.

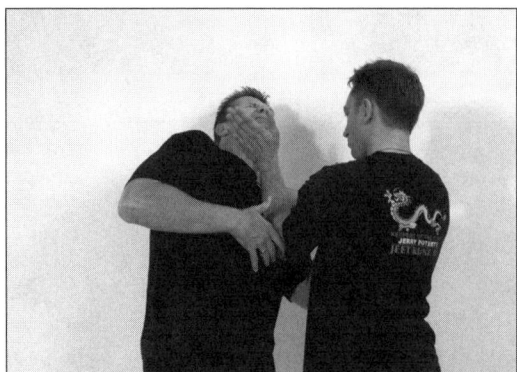

3.

Application from a Punch:

Octavio attempts a hit **(1)**. When Dimitri tries to counter with a lap sao grab, Octavio fires an eye jab **(2)**. When Octavio's path is obstructed again **(3)**, he switches his arm under to launch a throat slice with a trap **(4)**.

1.

2.

3.

4.

Application from a Pull:

Octavio and Dimitri clash arms **(1)**. Octavio attempts a Lap Sao grab **(2)**. Dimitri switches his hand inside **(3)** and flows to an Elbow Trap and Hit **(4)**.

1.

2.

3.

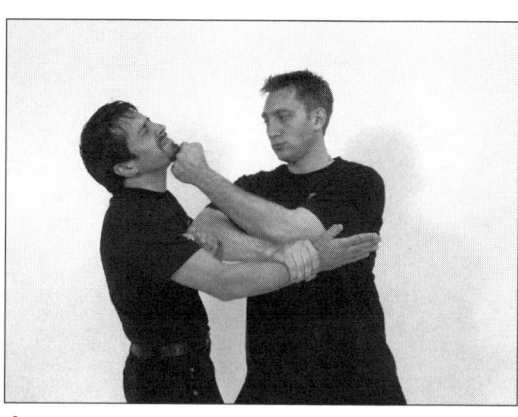

4.

Application from a Hook:

Ed throws a hook and Octavio covers **(1)**. Ed borrows the force of Octavio's cover to switch inside **(2)** and counters with his own strike **(3-4)**.

1.

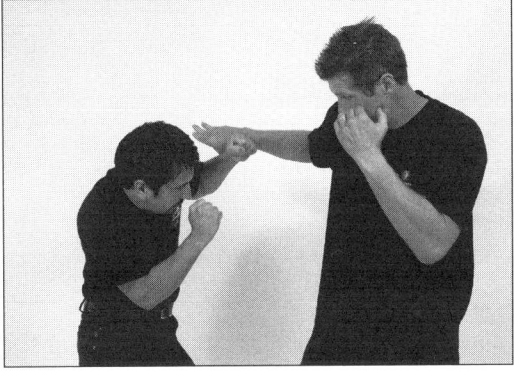
2.

3.

4.

These are just a few applications of the Switch Drill. The possibilities are endless, but it is the instantaneous tactile response for which we are aiming. Use your imagination with all these drills—let "IT" happen.

Jeet Kune Do Trapping—Reference Point Training

Now we move on to what Bruce called "Reference Point Training." It is a much more dynamic method of energy training than the drills, since we are adding elements of speed, power and (after the basics are mastered), surprise. It bears repeating that they are not fighting, although you will frequently find yourself in this range in a real encounter. Usually, people cannot apply this training, because they are attempting to do so at the wrong range.

Bruce Lee had no problems whatsoever in using trapping to fight. In fact, when he wanted to humiliate someone, he would say, "I'm going to move your right hand over to your left shoulder," and the opponent would just laugh. But sure enough, he could use Attack by Drawing (ABD) in this range so well that he got his enemy to move his own limbs. The ultimate goal of this training is to tie up the opponent's arms and hit him at will. At a later stage, you will use this training unconsciously everywhere in your body, attacking the opponent's centerline and dominating him completely. But first, it has to be learned in the arms. The reference point trapping starts with one person hitting and the other reacting passively with a block, parry or grab. After you are completely comfortable with this, it should graduate to the other person hitting or attacking after you initial movement. Finally, you should be able to use this in combat and in all ranges.

Trapping is one area where people just can't resist dazzling others with their speed. But many times their "victim" is not even trapped; he or she is just cooperating. Once you attain some skill, you should ask your training partner to hit you if he can. Of course, you already know how he will react. If he fails to do so, he will get hit. That is the beauty of this method. And Bruce was the "puppet master" when he used it on individuals. After the first few explosive moves, it looked as though his puppets had their strings cut! Remember, the purpose of trapping is to hit and control.

Reference Point Trapping—Rear Barriers

Bruce called blocks, parries, grabs, punches or anything that stopped an attack a "barrier." He then broke down trapping to your partner/opponent by responding either with the rear hand or punch, which he called "rear barriers;" or stopping your punch with his front hand or "front barrier." Since he always began with rear barriers, who are we to argue?

The first Reference Point is a rear cross parry. The punch is blocked and parried with the opponent's rear hand. It is done right to right or left to left. The pak sao is delivered with only enough force to clear the line to hit—no more, no less.

Right to Right

Jerry and Octavio are right to right **(1)**. Jerry attacks with a pak sao/punch and Octavio parries across his body with his rear hand **(2)**. Jerry rolls with the energy **(3)**, grabs and hits with a backfist **(4)**.

1.

2.

3.

4.

Here are some common mistakes.

Incorrect

Ed and Octavio square off **(1)**. Ed draws his hand back to pak sao **(2)**. (Don't pull back; fire from where the hand is.) When Octavio feels the disengagement, he pak sao's **(3)** and hits Ed.

1.

2.

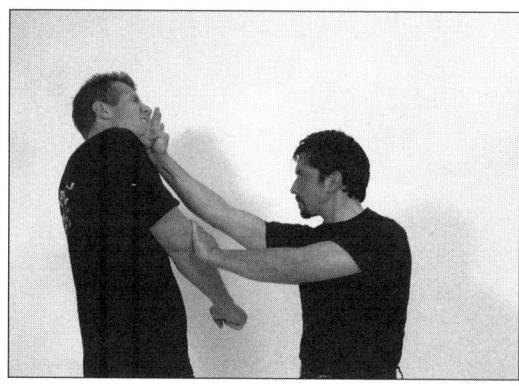

3.

Incorrect

Octavio obstructs Ed's arm **(1)**. Ed slaps the arm with a downward pak sao **(2)**. Octavio borrows the energy and rolls the arm around **(3)**. He finishes with a palm strike **(4)**.

1.

2.

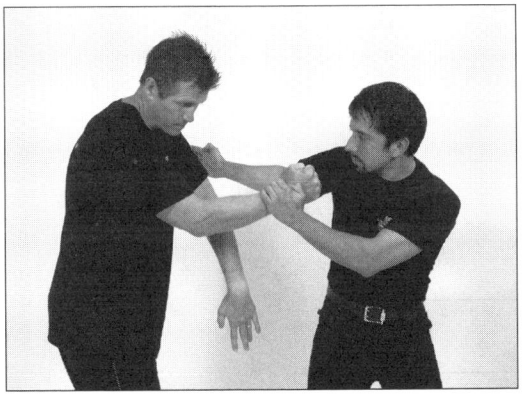
3.

4.

Incorrect

Ed tries to smack Octavio's arm out of the way **(1)**. Octavio hits! Why beat up limbs? It's a waste of energy **(2)**.

1.

2.

As with all movements in JKD, the last motion is the quickest. Explode with the last snap of the pak sao. Bruce used to quote Takuan, the Zen philosopher, by saying the explosions one felt along with the punch would "fetter the mind." In other words, the punch lands while your body is still busy reacting to the initial movement.

Correct Pak Sao

Ed and Octavio clash **(1)**. Ed pak sao's and punches simultaneously **(2)**.

1.

2.

First Progression

We now move on to the NPM principle again. In this progression, instead of rolling to a backfist when he parries with his rear hand, I punch instead.

Jerry and Octavio clash **(1)**. Jerry attacks with a pak sao and punch and Octavio parries **(2)**. Jerry fires a hit up the middle **(3)** and finishes with a hit and trap **(4)**.

1.

2.

3.

4.

Remember: Stay attached and trap (control) his body by keeping your elbows low. Punch up the center and destroy his axis! Don't let up on the pressure. Why give him another chance?

Second Progression

This time, the opponent punches back at different areas of your arm. This determines your response.

Jerry cannot get past Octavio's lead **(1)**. He pak sao's and punches and Octavio parries at Jerry's wrist **(2)**. Jerry fires a punch under his own arm **(3)**.

1.

2.

3.

Now, the pressure is closer to my elbow. When Jerry pak/punches, Octavio gives him pressure close to his elbow **(1)**. Jerry tan sao's and hits **(2)**. He flows to an inside pak sao and palm smash **(3)**.

1.

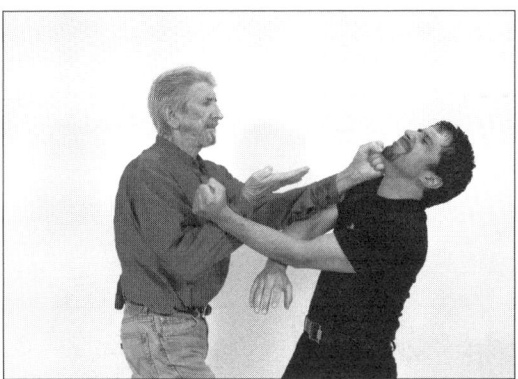

2.

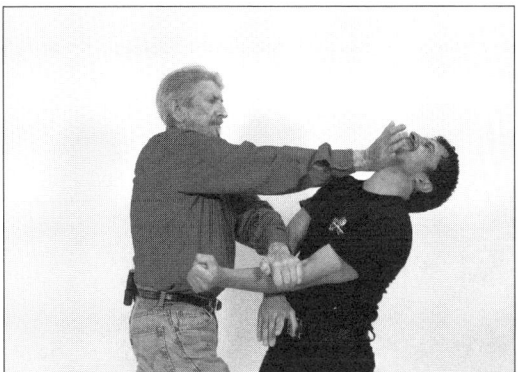

3.

Rear Barrier—Tan Sao

This is a classical response, a very refined movement, but it gives you the sensitivity to handle much more gross motion later on. These next few sequences are tie-ups or locks on the opponent.

When Jerry pak/punches, Octavio responds with a Tan Sao **(1)**. Jerry juts and hits with the rear hand **(2)**. He cross paks and hits while locking both arms **(3)**.

1.

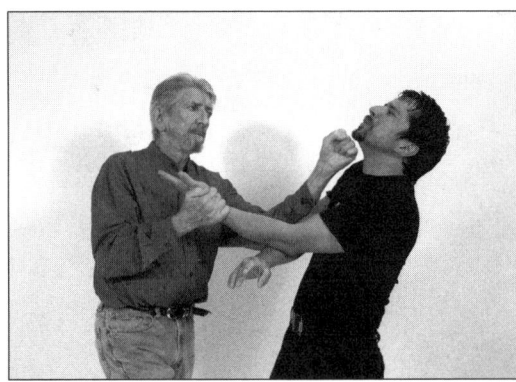

2.

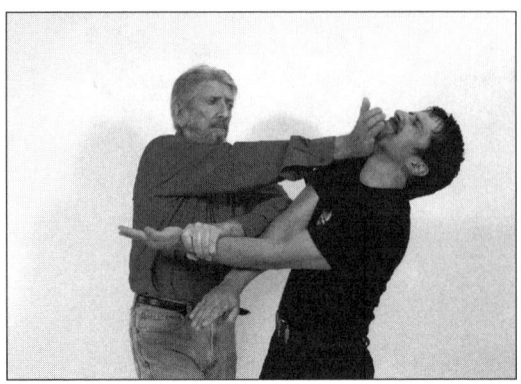

3.

Jerry attacks with a pak/punch and Octavio grabs his punch with his rear hand **(1)**. Jerry shoots a backfist, bounces off and grabs the hand that's grabbing **(2)**. He goes against the thumb to break the grab and circle **(3)**. Jerry shoots out a palm smash **(4)**.

1.

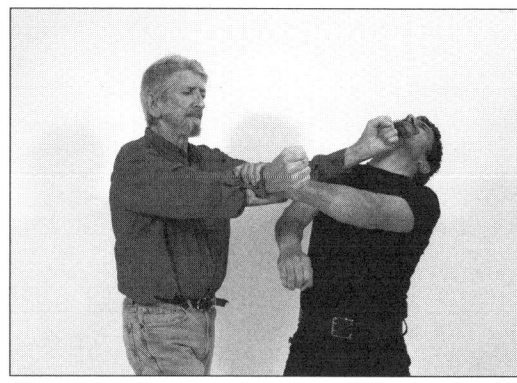

2.

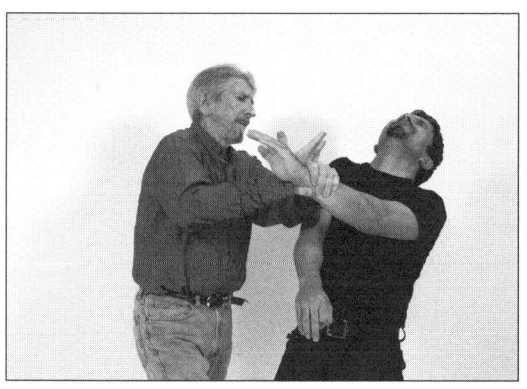

3.

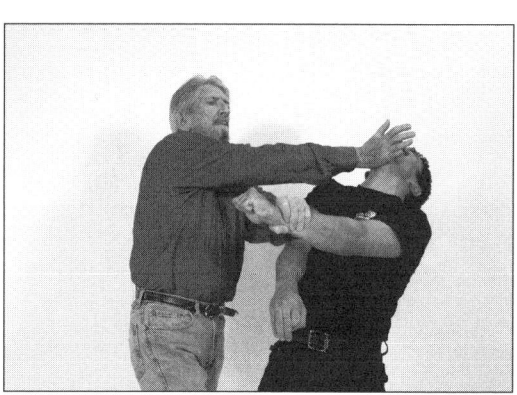

4.

Now, instead of using a Tan Sao, he *punches*. But it is the same energy he is giving you.

Jerry faces off with Octavio **(1)**. Instead of blocking or parrying, he fires a punch **(2)**. Jerry jut sao's and hits **(3)**, then traps Octavio's arms and hits **(4)**.

1.

2.

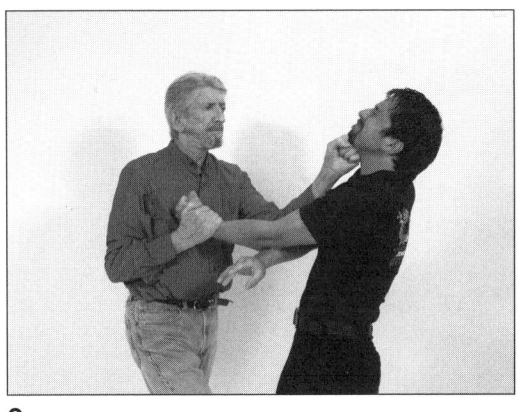

3.

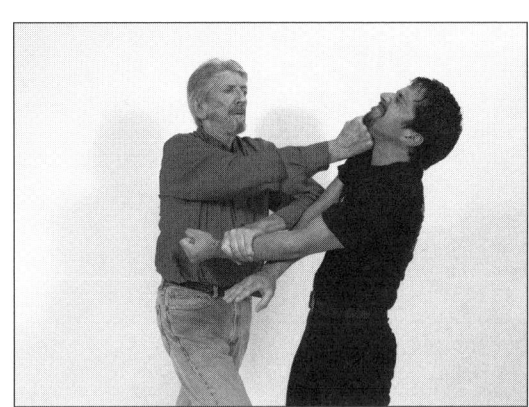

4.

Next, we will move on to front barrier. Now, your punch or strike is being obstructed in by the opponent's front hand.

Jerry's punch is obstructed by Dimitri **(1)**. Jerry tries to pak sao and punch, but Dimitri raises his front arm **(2)**. He borrows Dimitri's resistance to pull and backfist **(3)**. He follows up with a trap and throat slice **(4)**.

1.

2.

3.

4.

You may have noticed that I am using open-hand strikes, rather than punches. Bruce preferred this method of hitting, because *you don't lose a beat of time* opening and closing the hands. For example, if you have just trapped with a Lap Sao, your hand is already open. If you have to close your hand to make a fist to punch, you lose a precious moment (or beat) of time. I prefer open-hand strikes for a number of reasons: They deliver much more damage than fists; and they cover the face and block my opponent's eyesight. But the choice is yours.

The following two sequences employ the low hit. Some refer to these as high-low drills, but they are really *indirect attack* drills. You are learning to open lines on a skilled or much stronger opponent. As you will see, there has been a complete misunderstanding of the purpose of these drills and how to make them work.

Front Barrier—First Low Hit

When Jerry pak sao's and punches, Dimitri blocks high by raising his arms **(1)**. Once he gets him to lift his arms **(2)**, Jerry hits low (middle knuckle strikes are good). As the low one hits ("Fetter the Mind"), Jerry simultaneously hits high **(3)**.

1.

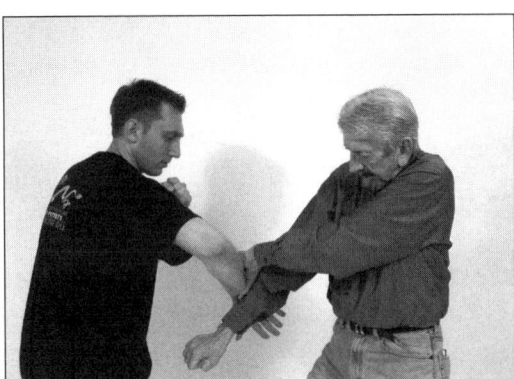

2.

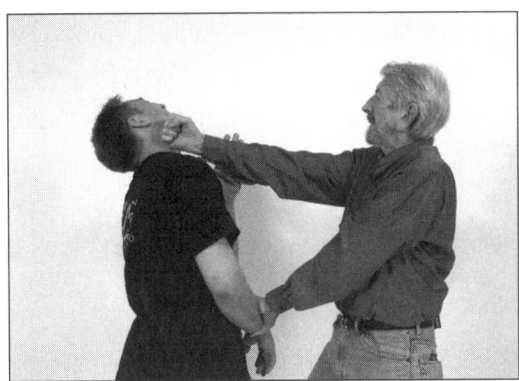

3.

Jerry raises Dimitri's arms by hitting high with a pak sao and punch **(1)**. When Dimitri follows the low hit down, Jerry traps and hits **(2)**. He finishes with a throat slice **(3)**.

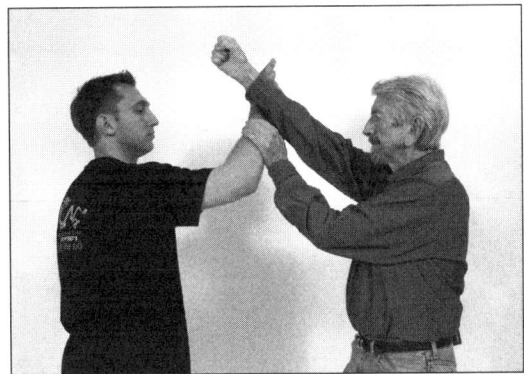

1.

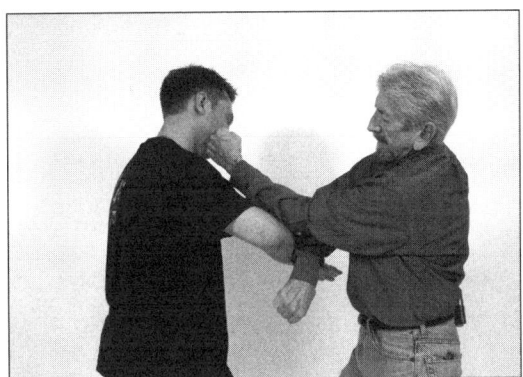

2.

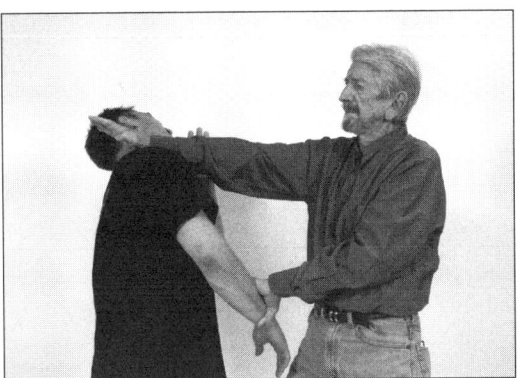

3.

Jerry attacks with a high pak sao punch combination **(1)**. When he follows the low hit down, Jerry traps **(2)** with a waum pak (cross-pak), slices to the throat **(3)** and fires another **(4)**.

1.

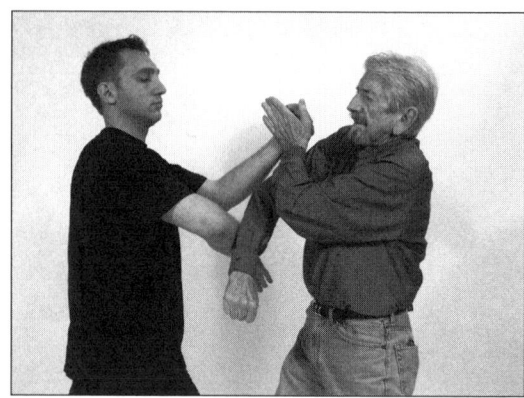

2.

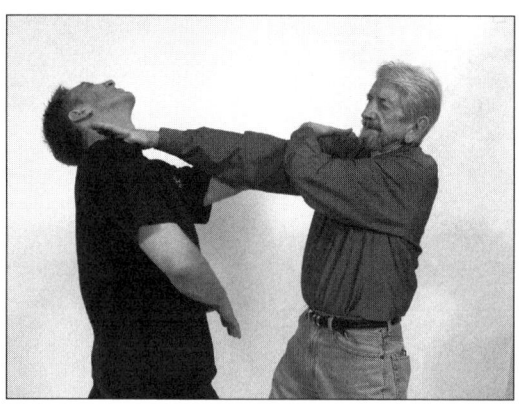

3.

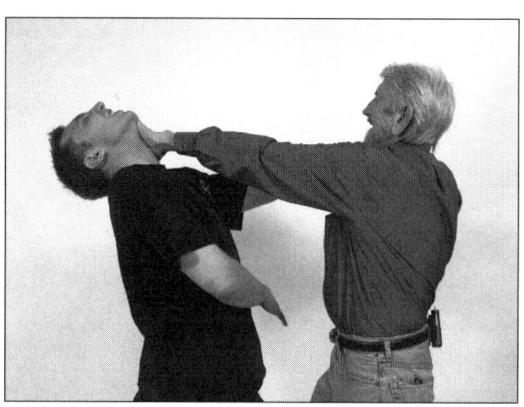

4.

Front Barrier—Low Parry With Rear Hand

Jerry pak sao's and punches high, drawing Dimitri's arms up **(1)**. When he hits low, Dimitri blocks with his *rear* hand **(2)**. Jerry uses the energy to circle around with a jao sao hit while trapping with his left **(3)**. Jerry cross-traps and hits with a palm strike **(4)**.

1.

2.

3.

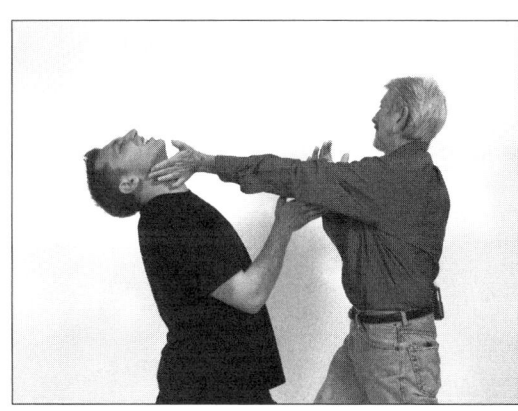
4.

Front Barrier—They Hit

This time, when Jerry attacks high with a pak sao and punch **(1)**, Dimitri launches a rear punch **(2)**. Jerry bobs and hits inside **(3)**. Then finishes with an elbow **(4)**.

1.

2.

3.

4.

When I trained with Bruce Lee, he used these attacks to open up lines or lanes for hitting, kicking, etc. He could use misdirection to get you to open up your own defenses. At long range, he did not even need to trap or tie up; he could control your arms without touching you. The following shows this:

Dimitri and Ed square off **(1)**. Dimitri drops his body to feint a low hit **(2)**. Ed goes for the bait and drops his front hand **(3)**. Dimitri pins the arm and hits **(4)**.

1.

2.

3.

4.

The point is that he learned this application from the energy training, and used it to suit his own purposes. The world is different today. Real fights now occur much closer in, rather than at a longer distance sparring range. No matter how or in what range you fight, these reference point attacks will be prove useful indeed. The following are just applications in boxing range, etc. Remember, these are primarily *indirect attacks*.

Dimitri and Ed square off **(1)**. Ed fires a jab and notices that Dimitri blocks **(2)**. He fires low knowing that his opponent will follow **(3)**. Ed traps and hits **(4)**, then cuts through Dimitri's parry with a punch **(5)**. Ed slices another punch through Dimitri's parry **(6)**.

1.

2.

3.

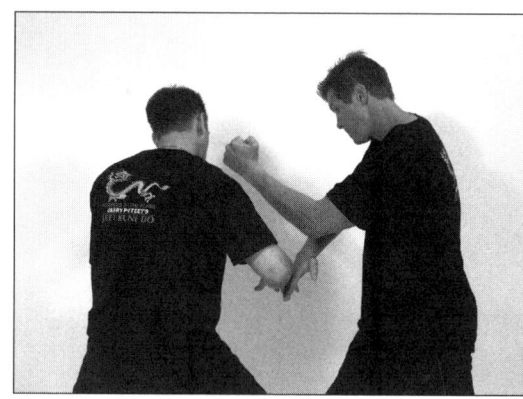

4.

5.

6.

Using misdirection, Dimitri punches high **(1),** gets his opponent to follow his low hit **(2)**, then shifts off-line with an uppercut **(3)**.

1.

2.

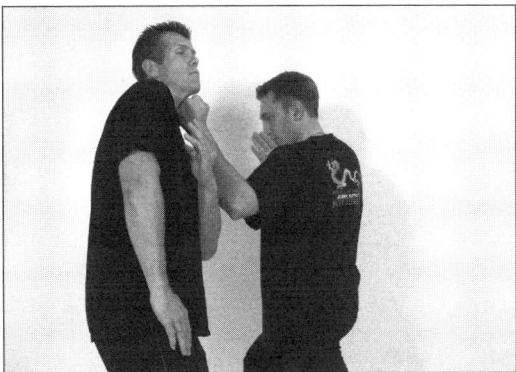

3.

Dimitri faces off with Ed **(1)**. He opens the line by shooting an eye jab outside Ed's lead arm **(2)**. When Ed's arm follows it out, Dimitri switches the eye jab inside **(3)**.

1.

2.

3.

Ed and Octavio square off **(1)**. Ed shoots a high eye jab to open the line **(2)**. When Octavio resists with outside pressure, Ed switches inside with a punch **(3)**. He flows to a low groin strike **(4)**, a vertical elbow smash **(5)** and an arm break **(6)**.

1.

2.

3.

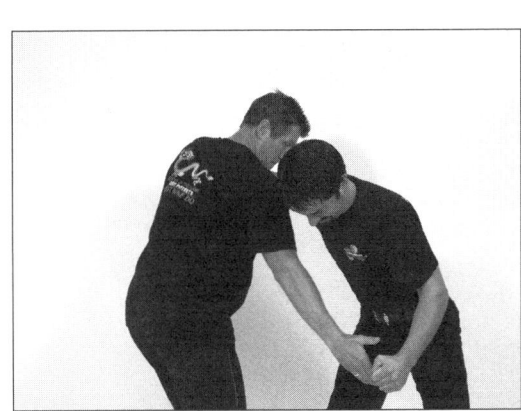

4.

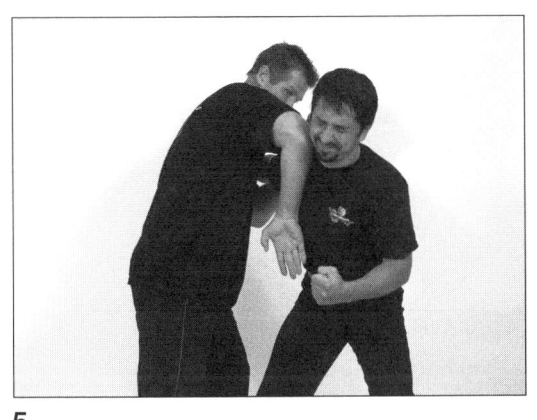

5.

6.

Octavio and Ed face each other **(1)**. Octavio throws a wide hook **(2)**. Ed takes the bait and blocks with both hands **(3)**. Octavio bounces off the block to hit outside **(4)**, trap and hit again **(5)**.

1.

2.

3.

4.

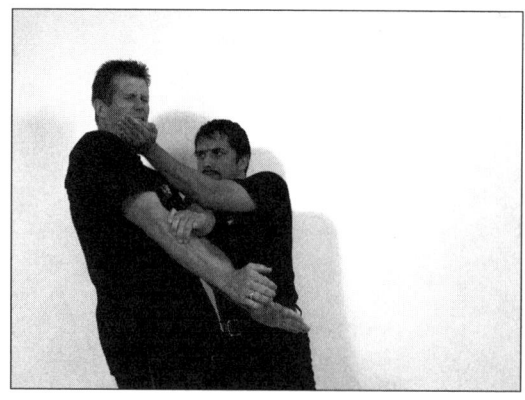
5.

CHI SAO

By Jerry Poteet, with Fran Joseph

The final stage in Jeet Kune Do energy training is Chi Sao. Everything you have previously learned is now put to the test. As you can see from the pictures, you are now much *closer* to your opponent. Everything is happening so fast there is no time to think—which is exactly the point. Much like professional sports, you are over-speed training, so that the common punches, strikes, knees and takedowns will become second nature. With this heightened awareness, you will find yourself pre-empting most of your opponent's attacks, and as Bruce explained, "Intercepting his intentions." This section will explore a few of the drills and applications.

Chi Sao training is a life-long endeavor. You can never develop enough tactile awareness, or sensitivity to your opponent's touch. Also, every individual has a different "feel," or pressure to his limbs. (Yes, Chi Sao encompasses the entire body. But for the purposes of this book, it is first learned with the arms). It joins both hemispheres of the brain; in the beginning, when you think of hitting with the right hand, the left goes soft, and vice versa. Gradually, both hands work together in harmony, yin and yang seamlessly connected.

Ultimately, you can use Chi Sao to develop awareness past martial arts. You heighten the rest of the senses, so you are a complete being. But that is a topic for another time.

Structure

The most important element of Chi Sao is proper structure. Everything flows from this. Without it, Chi Sao is just a grab bag of tricks. Structure is the most important element when you first learn Chi Sao. Only when the structure becomes part of you, when you are not thinking of "right hand," "left hand," or are losing the pressure or sensitivity of either, can you progress to the next level.

When Bruce taught me and he felt my structure was good, we did not start hitting. Instead, we started switching. This switching is starting with the left hand and switching inside without losing contact with your opponent's arm. You should be able to maintain *forward pressure* throughout the movement. Next, switch outside with the right hand, again without losing contact with correct pressure. Chi Sao is not just with one structure; the right hand is not always inside and the left is not always outside. It is constantly changing, which ultimately is to your advantage.

If an instructor or teacher starts you off with, this method creates bad habits and usually makes the student "gun shy" and always assume a purely defensive mode. Here's how to develop good structure in Chi Sao training.

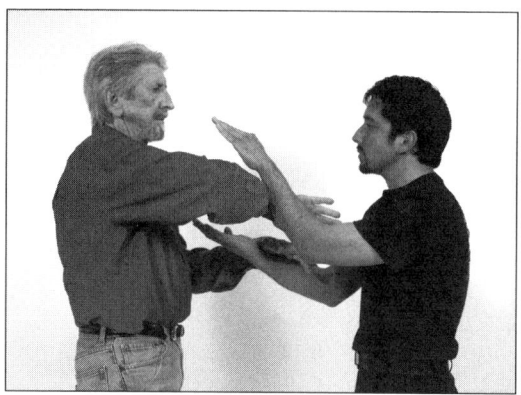

You can see that the elbow is slightly higher than the wrist in the Boang Sao position (Jerry).

The fingers are pointed at the center.

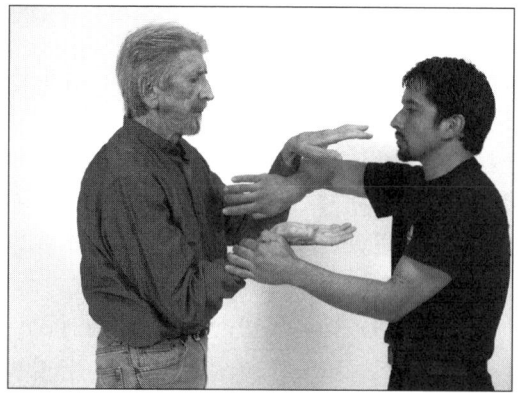
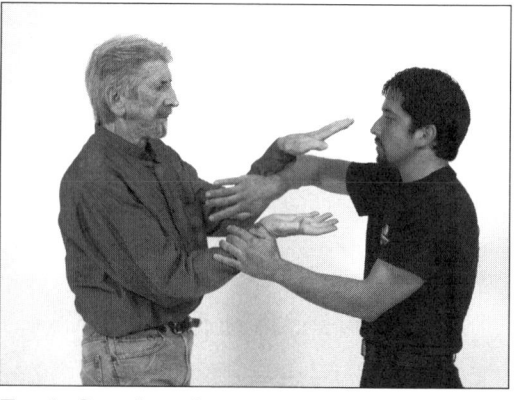

The elbow is in toward center on the outside hand.

Fook Sao has been changed to Bill Gee and Jut Sao.

The very first hit in Chi Sao, the inside right-hand hit **(1)**, is very difficult to stop, because it is so close to the target (for practice we go to the chest). This hit simulates a common scenario in actual confrontations—the push or shove with a punch **(2)**. Students always want to move on before they can effectively deal with this hit. Yet, it is probably the most important aspect of Chi Sao. Be sure you can neutralize the right-hand inside hit before you progress to other attacks.

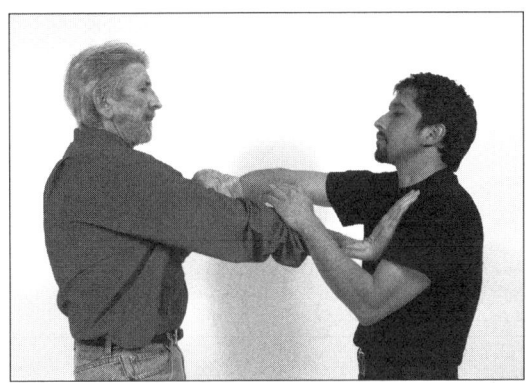

1.

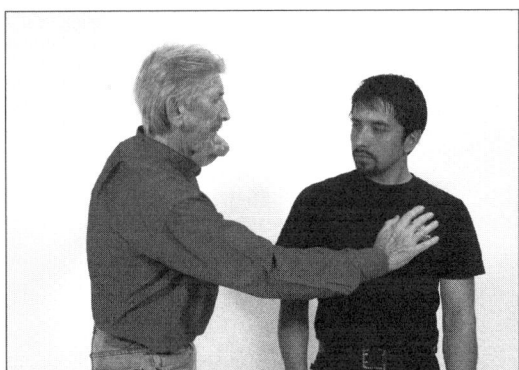

2.

Indirect Attack

When Jerry tries to hit Octavio inside, he drops his elbow with cross-energy pressure to stop the hit **(1)**. Jerry just transfers the energy and continues the pressure to a cross-grab **(2)**. Without stopping, he flows to a hit **(3)** with the grab, (trap).

1.

2.

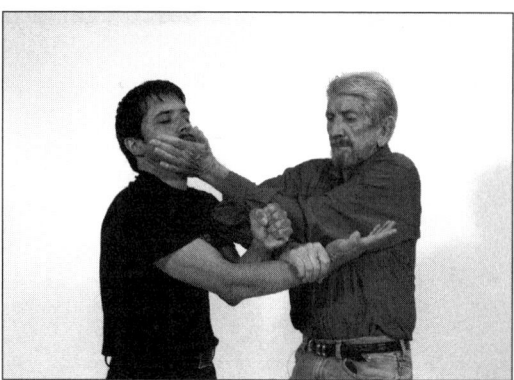

3.

Inside Lap Sao Switch

Jerry and Octavio roll in Chi Sao **(1)**. Jerry does an inside lap sao **(2)**. When he does, Octavio switches with the pull and stops his hit with his own **(3)**.

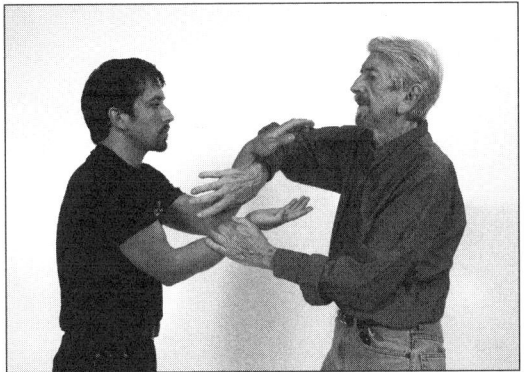

1.

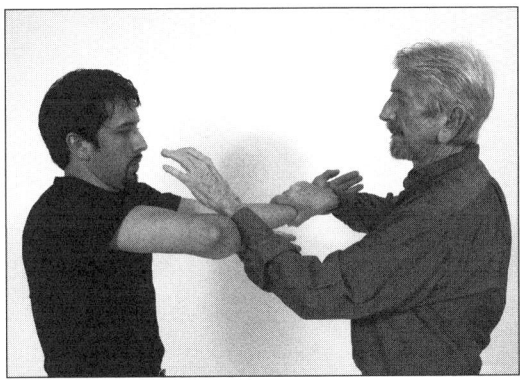

2.

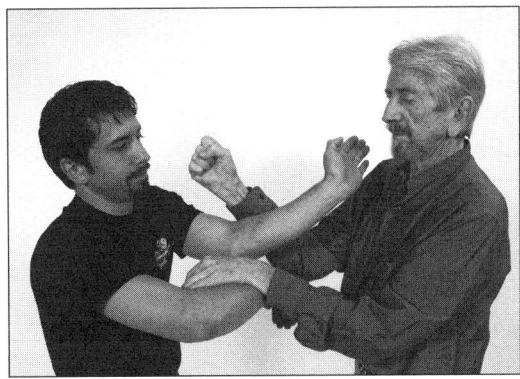

3.

Cutting the Sphere in Half

From Chi Sao, Jerry grabs Octavio's hand **(1)**. He rolls the left hand under and hits **(2)**. Octavio drops his elbow to stop the attack **(3)**. Jerry rolls out and fires a backfist over the arm **(4)**.

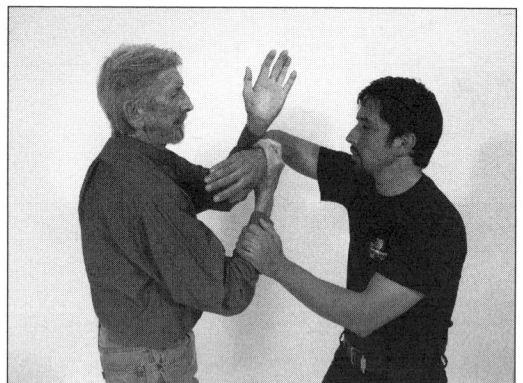
1.

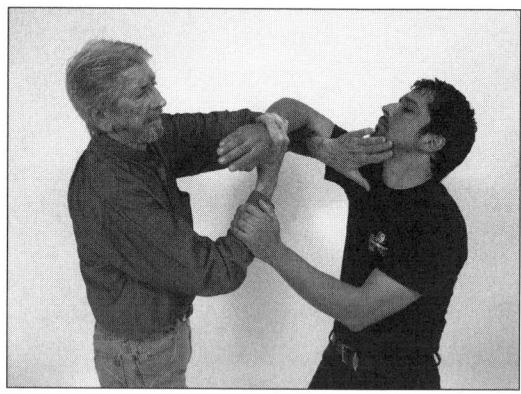
2.

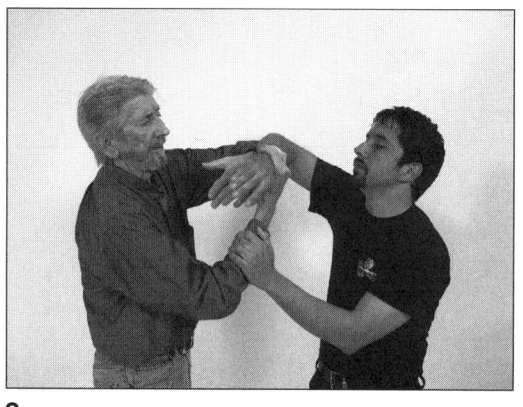
3.

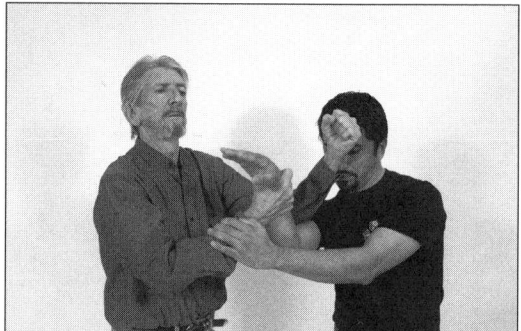
4.

BY JERRY POTEET, WITH FRAN JOSEPH

The "Whip"

Jerry prepares to attack in Chi Sao **(1)**. He whips to his right and hits inside **(2)**. When Octavio resists, he strikes inside **(3)**. Jerry uses a pull to trap and a push to punch **(4)**. He finishes with a slice and trap **(5)**.

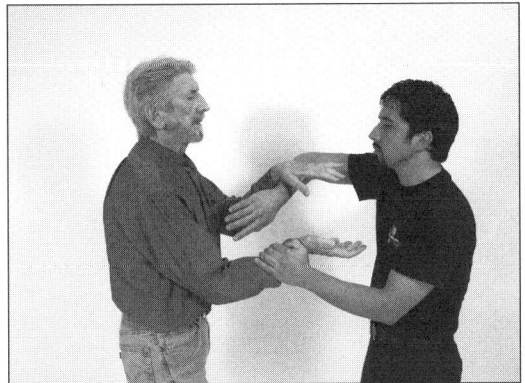

1.

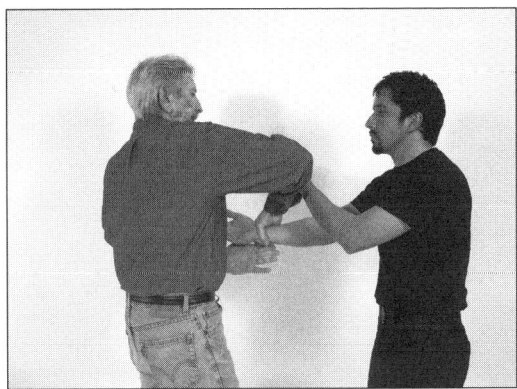

2.

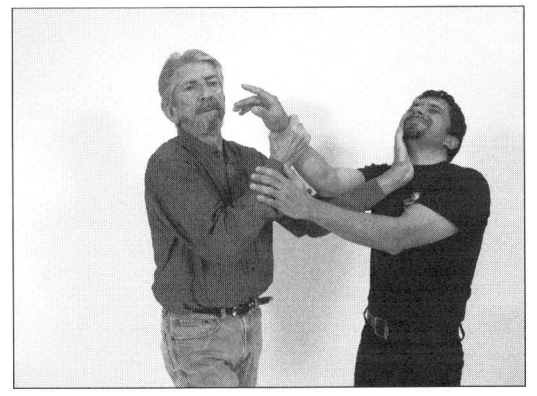

3.

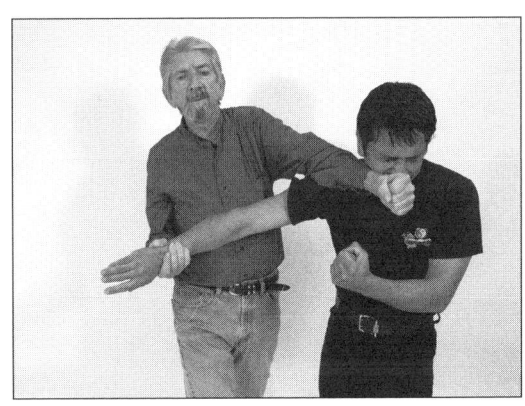

4.

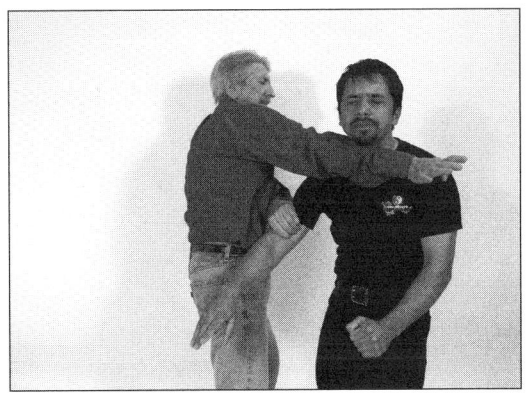

5.

Cross-Pak Attack

Jerry fetters the mind with a Bil Gee thrust **(1)**. When he feels an opening, he cross-pak's and boang sao's to obstruct both arms **(2)**. Jerry fires an open palm strike to Octavio's head **(3)**.

1.

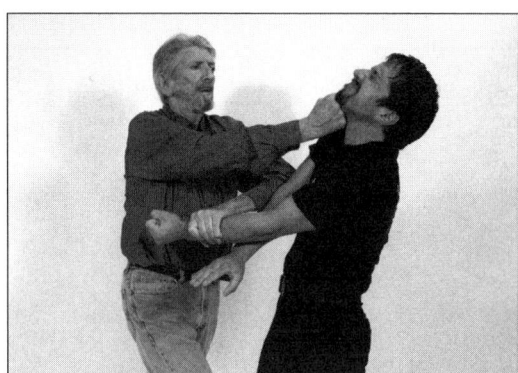

2.

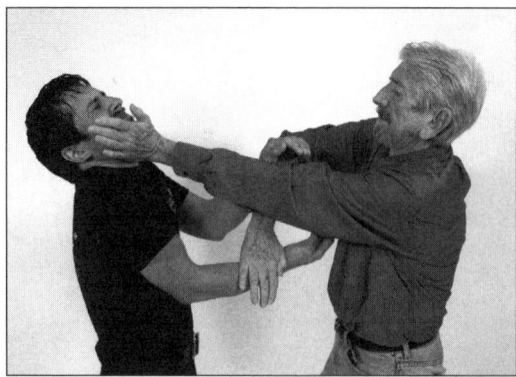

3.

Outside Tan Sao—Indirect Attack

Remember, *every* movement in Jeet Kune Do is aggressive. The Tan Sao, like all movements, is an attack, and *not* a block! This is another example of Indirect Attack, because we are drawing a response with the first movement.

Jerry threatens Octavio with a Tan Sao spear **(1)**. When Octavio tenses up, he lap sao's and throws a backfist **(2)**. He finishes with a pull and palm strike **(3)**.

1.

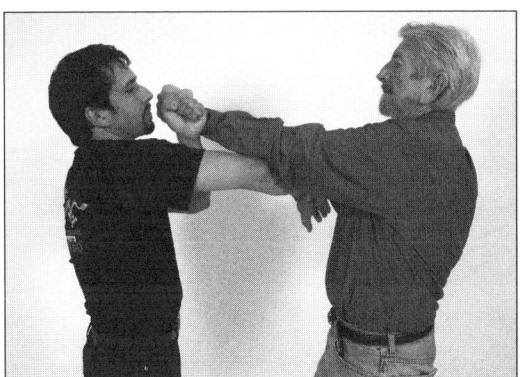
2.

3.

Now, let's examine several common mistakes in Chi Sao.

Incorrect—Leaving Both Hands Vulnerable

Jerry and Octavio prepare to Chi Sao **(1)**. When Octavio attempts a Tan Sao, he leaves his other hand up instead of dissolving **(2)**. Jerry grabs and locks both hands **(3)**, then fires between both arms with a punch to the throat **(4)**.

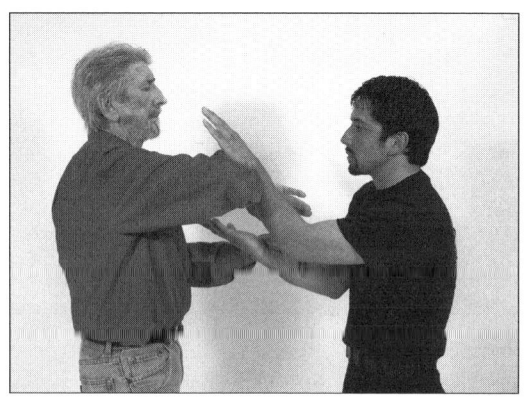

1.

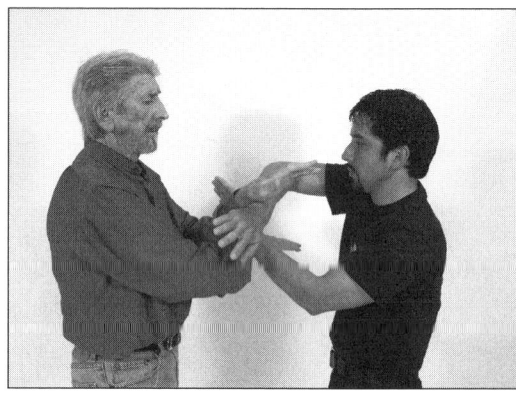

2.

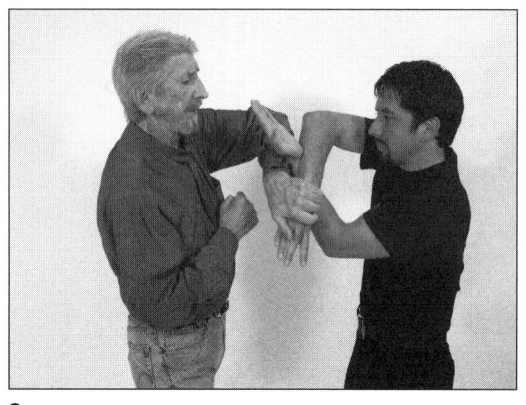

3.

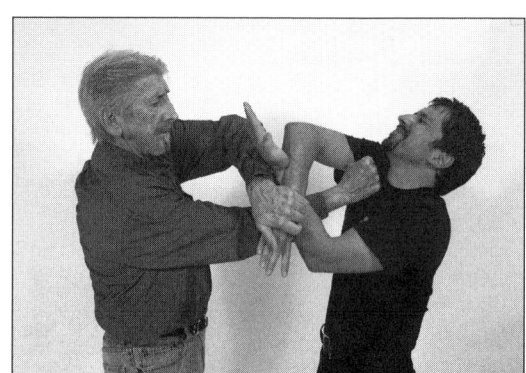

4.

Incorrect—Passive Moves

This is a prime example of violating the No Passive Moves rule. In other words, why beat up an arm?

Octavio and Ed roll in Chi Sao **(1)**. Ed disengages and breaks structure **(2)**. He parries Octavio's arm **(3)**. As soon as Octavio feels "emptiness," he controls and hits **(4)**, then traps with a downward elbow strike **(5)**.

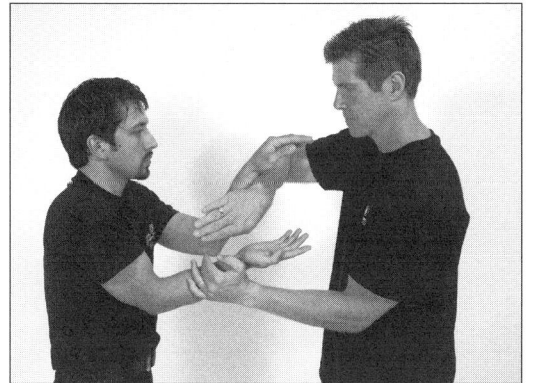
1.

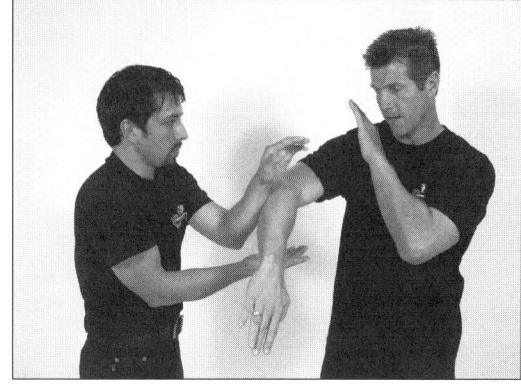
2.

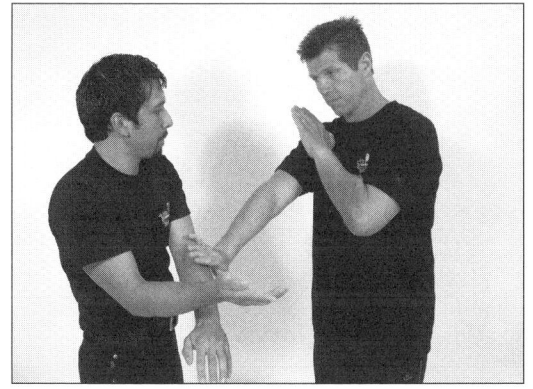
3.

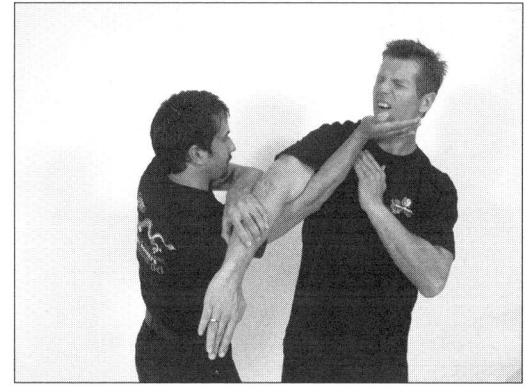
4.

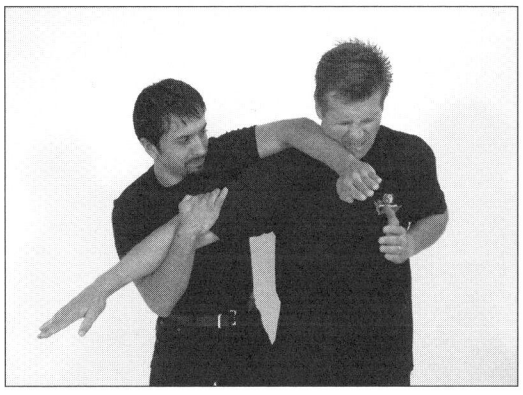
5.

Incorrect—Grapple Counter

Octavio and Ed roll in Chi Sao **(1)**. Ed breaks out of structure and attempts to grapple **(2)**. Octavio maintains pressure and structure and hits him on the back of the neck **(3)**. He keeps Ed's downward energy going with a neck pull **(4)**. And finishes with a knee smash to the face **(5)**.

1.

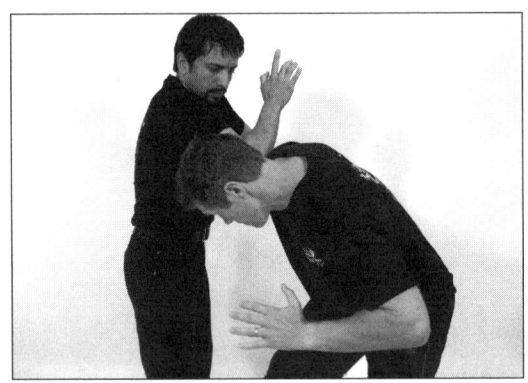

2.

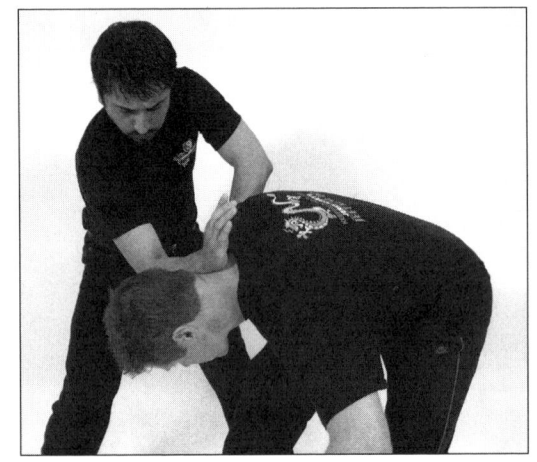

3.

4.

5.

Incorrect—Parrying Instead of Hitting

Octavio and Ed are in Chi Sao **(1)**. Ed breaks out and parries Octavio's arm **(2)**. He parries again **(3)** and parries again **(4)**.

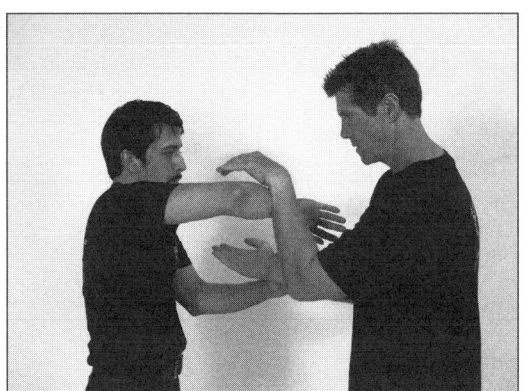

1.

2.

3.

4.

Correct—Hit

This time, when he prepares to triple parry **(1)**, Octavio feels the lack of pressure and hits **(2)**. He then controls with a trap and hit **(3)**.

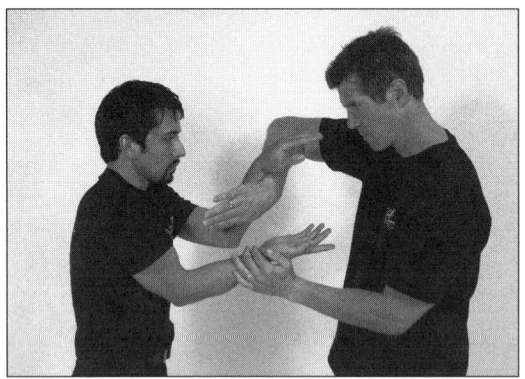

1.

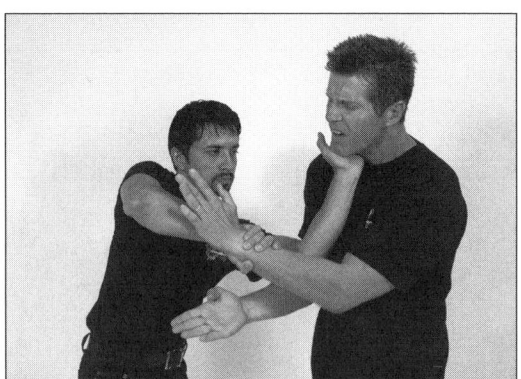

2.

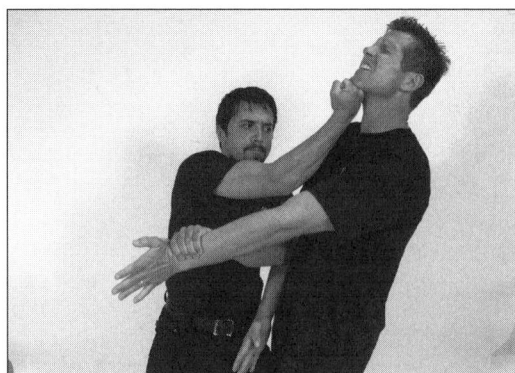

3.

Incorrect

Octavio and Ed roll **(1)**. Octavio makes a direct attack without waiting for a response **(2)**. Ed counterattacks with a trap and slice to the neck **(3)**, then finishes with a control and punch **(4)**.

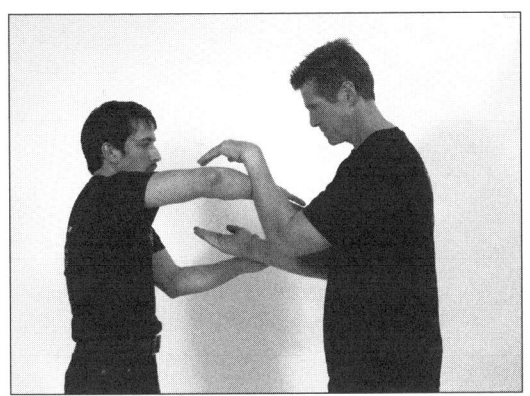
1.

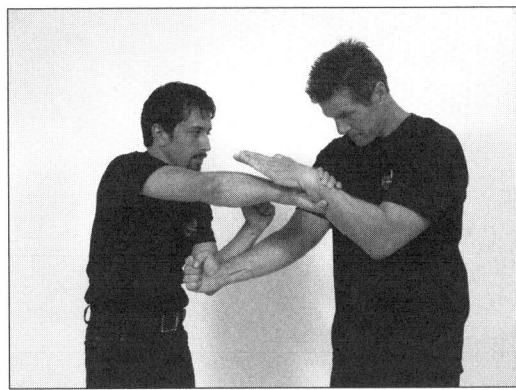
2.

3.

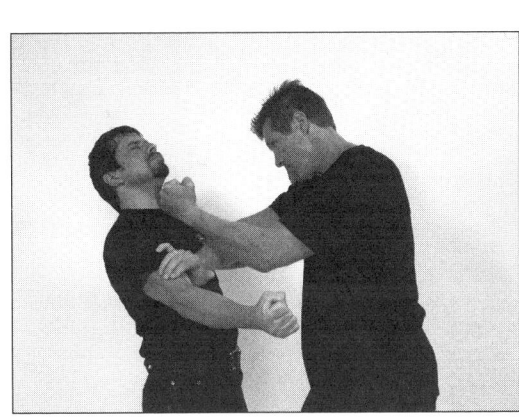
4.

Correct—Intercept

Octavio and Ed roll in Chi Sao **(1)**. Ed attempts an elbow **(2)**. Octavio intercepts it with his own elbow strike **(3)**.

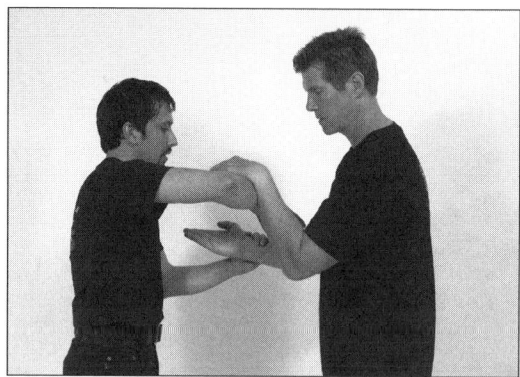

1.

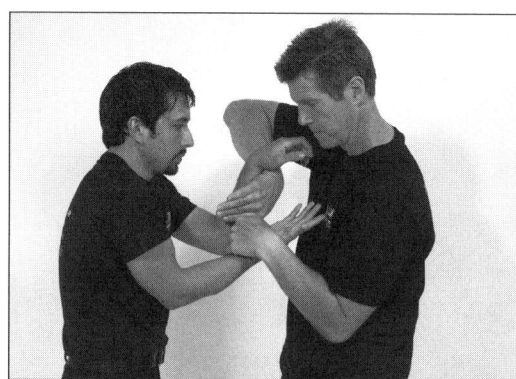

2.

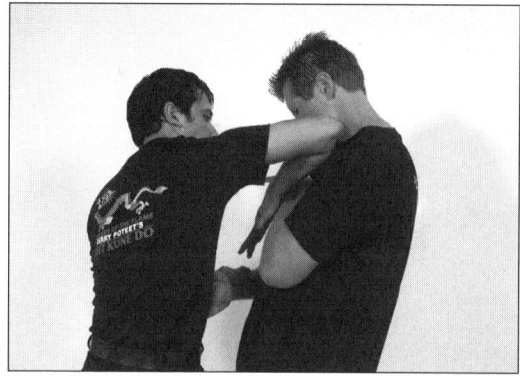

3.

Incorrect—Don't Disengage

Ed starts to withdraw his arm up high **(1)**. When he tries to throw a hook Octavio feels "emptiness" and springs forward with a hit **(2)**. He finishes with a trap and choke **(3)**.

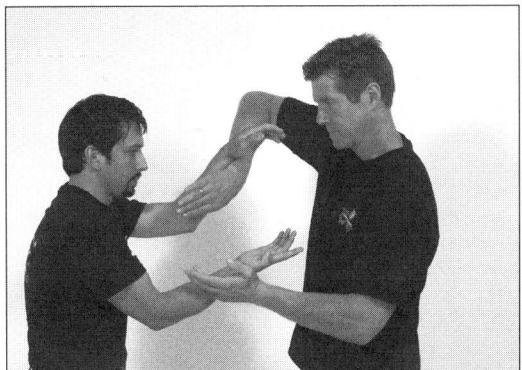

1.

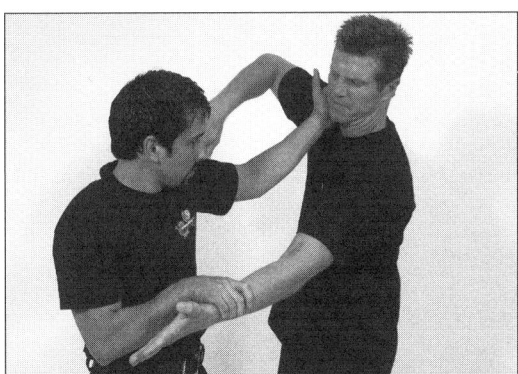

2.

3.

Incorrect—Pull On Arms

When Ed tries to muscle Octavio with a yank **(1)**, Octavio goes to the open side with an elbow **(2)**. He follows up with an uppercut **(3)**.

1.

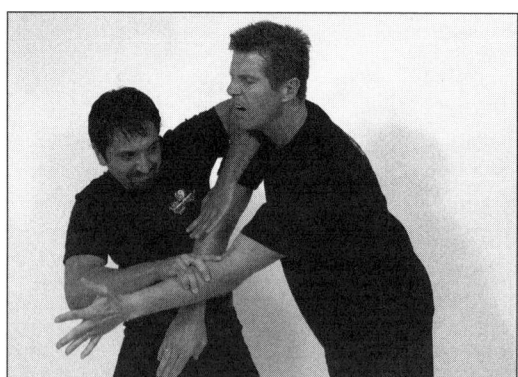

2.

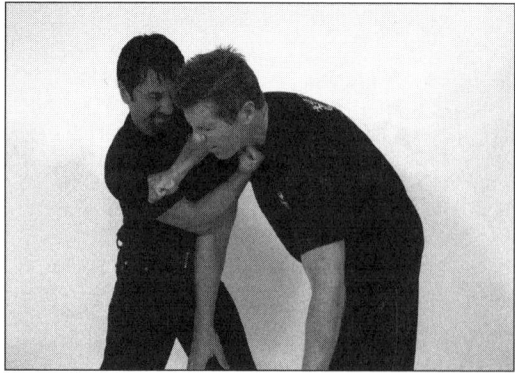

3.

Incorrect—Neck Wrench

Ed attempts to pull Octavio's head down **(1)**. Octavio borrows the pull to go in with a palm smash **(2)**. He grabs Ed's neck **(3)** and knees him in the head **(4)**. He then uses the rebound to kick his leg **(5)**. If Ed manages to block the knee down **(6)**, Octavio uses the energy to kick his leg **(7)**.

1.

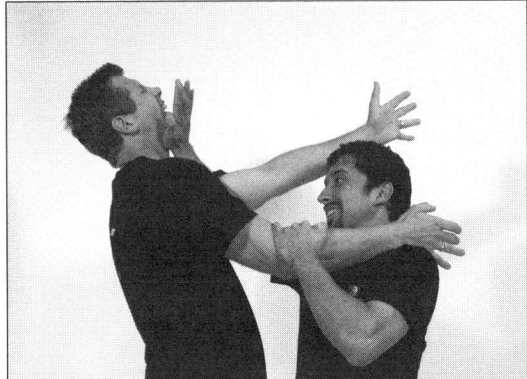

2.

3.

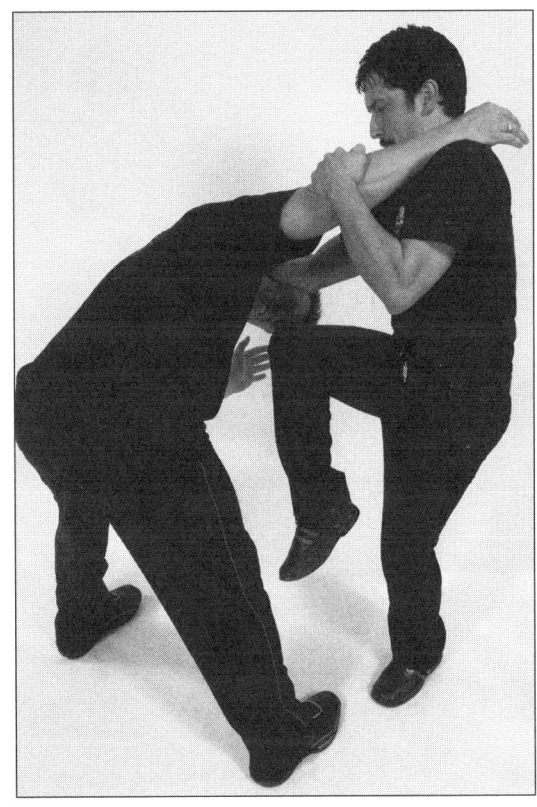

4.

5.

6.

7.

When someone does not have Chi Sao, it has been my experience that he reverts to familiar movements. This is almost always a mistake.

Incorrect—Wrestler's Swim

Ed prepares to attack Octavio **(1)**. Ed uses a swim arm to get a tackle **(2)**. Octavio follows his energy down with an elbow smash **(3)**.

1.

2.

3.

Incorrect—Judo Throw

1.

Octavio attempts a throw **(1)**. Ed goes with the energy by relaxing his arm **(2)**, switches behind with an eye jab **(3)**...

Continued on next page.

2.

3.

and shifts back to attack **(4)**. He finishes with a knee to the tailbone **(5)**.

4.

5.

Incorrect—One Hand Goes Soft

Ed senses Octavio's pressure **(1)**. Ed feels Octavio's tan sao lose forward pressure **(2)**. He uses the opening to hook **(3)**.

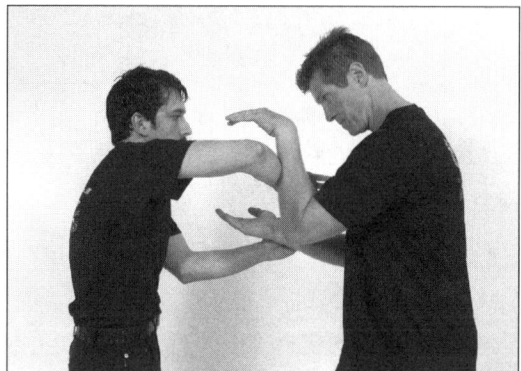

1.

2.

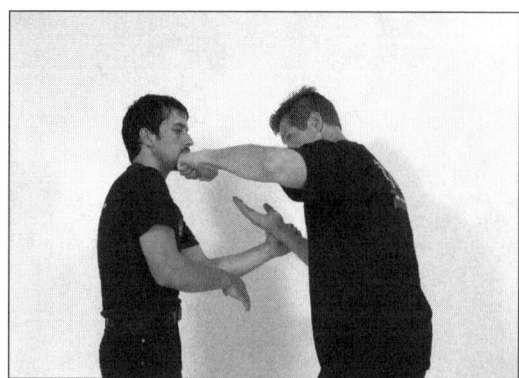

3.

Fitting in with a Fighter's Energy

Even if you end up on the ground, you still have ample opportunities to hit. Whatever you apply standing up, works just the same in any other position.

1.

Octavio attempts a hair pull and grab **(1)**.
Ed goes with the force and hits **(2)**.
And hits again **(3)**.

2.

3.

Ed and Octavio struggle **(1)**. Octavio elbows in the gap **(2),** flows to a reverse headlock **(3)** and finishes with a takedown **(4)**.

1.

2.

3.

4.

When Octavio tries to headlock and grab **(1)**, Ed feels his energy and turns it around on him **(2)**. He drops to one knee **(3)** and has total control **(4)**.

1.

2.

3.

4.

Fitting in with a Groundfighter's Energy

When Octavio attempts a groin kick **(1)**, Ed grabs the leg **(2)**. The fight goes to the ground **(3)**. When Ed draws back to punch **(4)**, Octavio shoots an eye jab **(5)**.

1.

2.

3.

4.

5.

He elbows Ed in the groin **(6)**, fires another punch **(7)**, slices his throat **(8)** and manages to roll over and out **(9)**. Before Ed can recover **(10)**, Octavio punches the groin **(11)**.

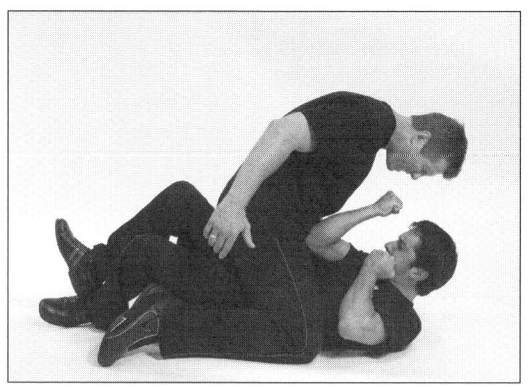

6.

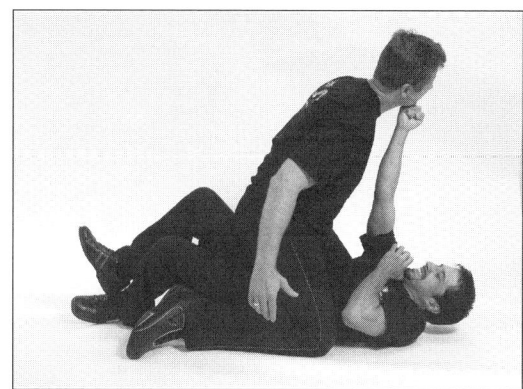

7.

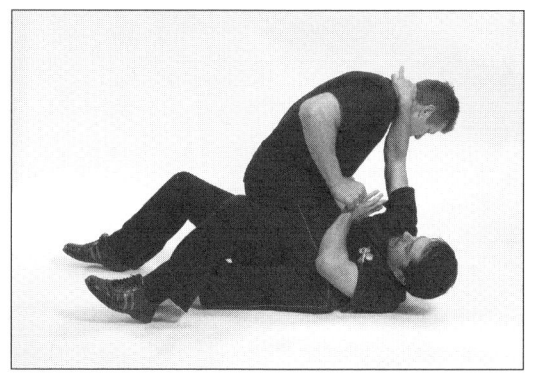

8.

9.

10.

11.

Ed is on top drawing back to punch Octavio **(1)**. Octavio shifts to the side and hooks him in the groin **(2)**. Octavio attempts an arm bar **(3)**. When he applies pressure with the arm bar, he leaves his groin exposed **(4)**.

1.

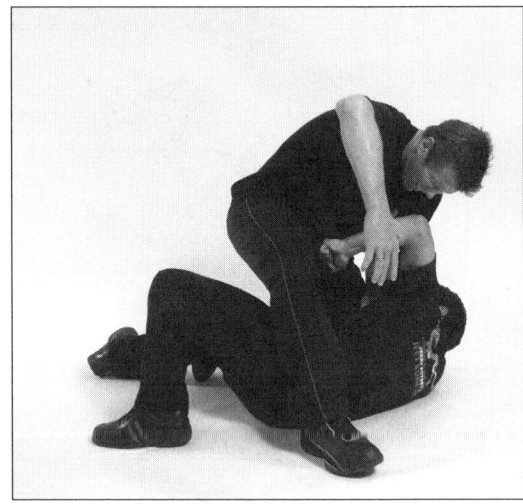

2.

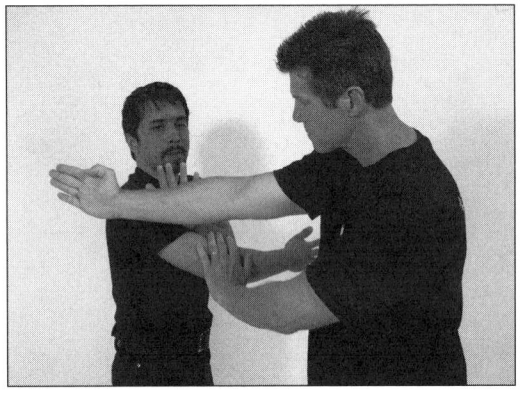

3.

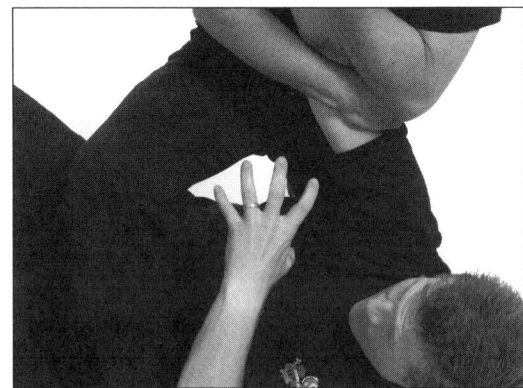

4.

Ed hits **(5)**, rolls off and over **(6)**. He then hits to the throat **(7)** and ties him up with control **(8)**.

5.

6.

7.

8.

Ed attempts to step over Octavio **(1)**. Octavio kicks to the groin **(2)** and attacks Ed with an eye jab **(3)**.

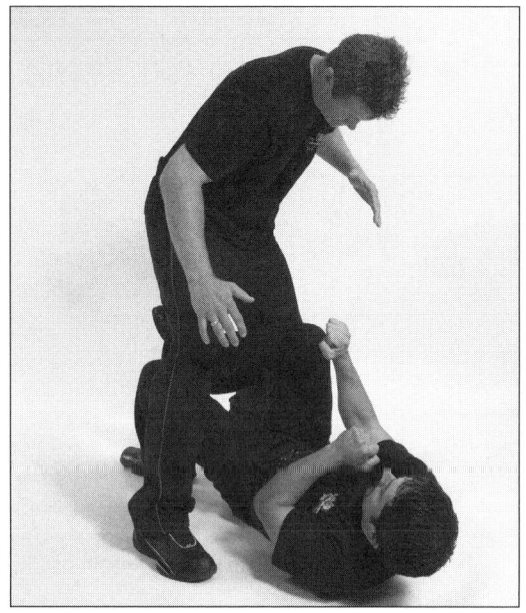
1.

2.

3.

Ed is on top and preparing to hit **(1)**. Octavio hits the eye **(2)** and breaks the arm as he rolls off **(3)**. He elbows to the face as he rolls on top **(4)** and finishes with a downward elbow to the groin **(5)**.

1.

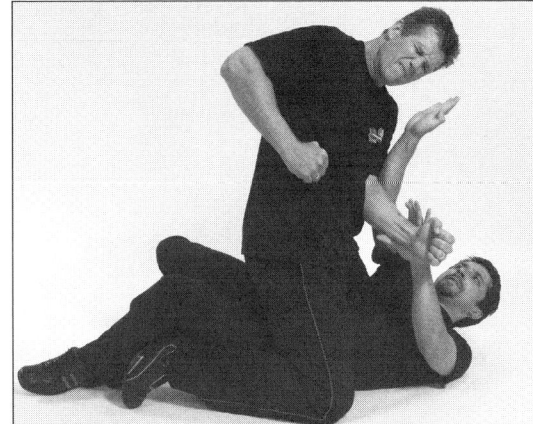

2.

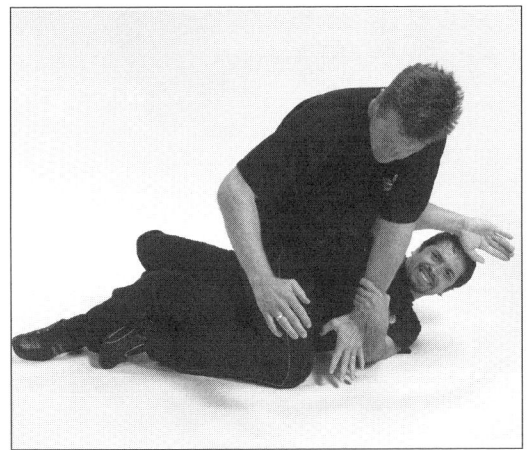

3.

4.

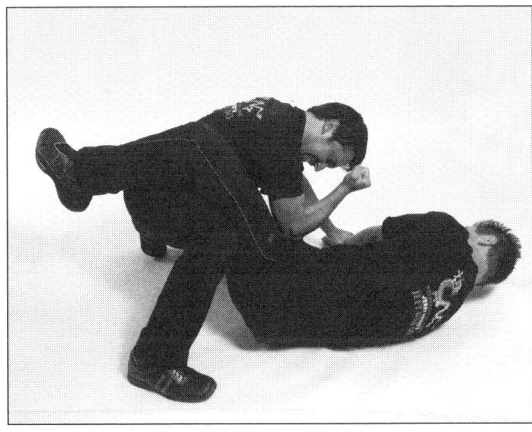

5.

Energy Responses to Threats

Ed counters Dimitri's kick with a leg block **(1)**. Dimitri follows his energy in and closes with a hit **(2)**. Dimitri attempts to shove and hit **(3)**. Ed lets the push turn him and hits immediately with a palm heel to the face **(4)**.

1.

2.

3.

4.

Dimitri pulls Ed from behind **(1)**. Instead of resisting, Ed turns toward Dimitri **(2)**. He hits with a backfist **(3)** and follows up with a cross **(4)**.

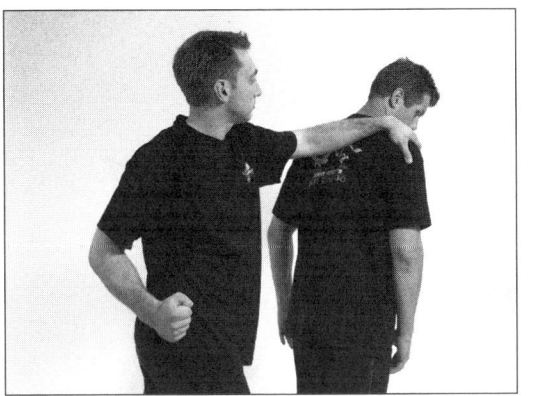
1.

2.

3.

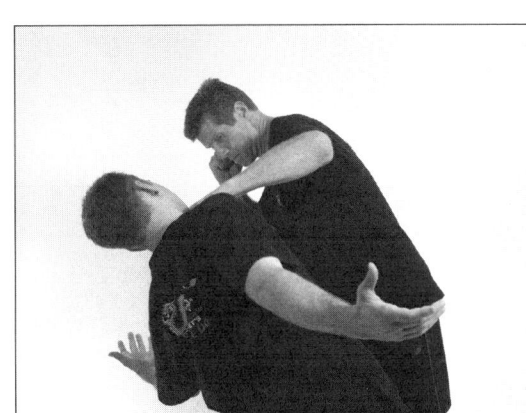
4.

Ed attempts a leg bar on Octavio **(1)**. Octavio kicks his groin **(2)**.

1.

2.

Ed attempts to get Octavio in the guard **(1)**. Octavio straight blasts the groin and every target **(2)**. As Ed attempts to lift up **(3)**, Octavio uses his energy and drops down with an elbow smash **(4)**.

1.

2.

3.

4.

Ed attempts to grab Octavio's leg **(1)**. Octavio launches with a kick to the groin **(2)**. Octavio continues with the leg pressure and sends him over **(3)**.

1.

2.

3.

Ed and Octavio find themselves in one Chi Sao position **(1)**. Doesn't matter if you are on the ground **(2)**. You can trap **(3)**. And hit **(4)**.

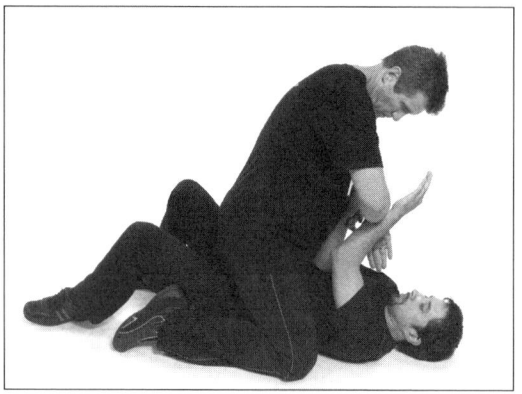
1.

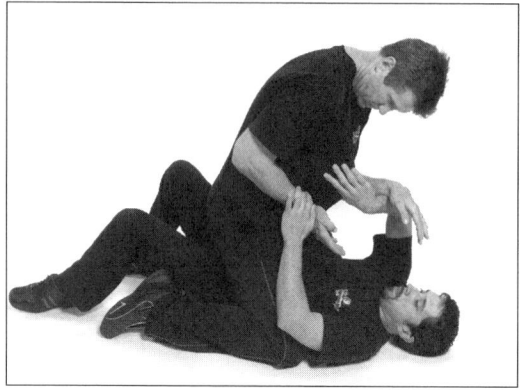
2.

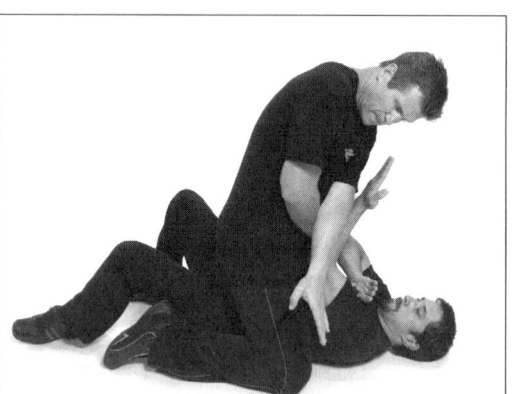
3.

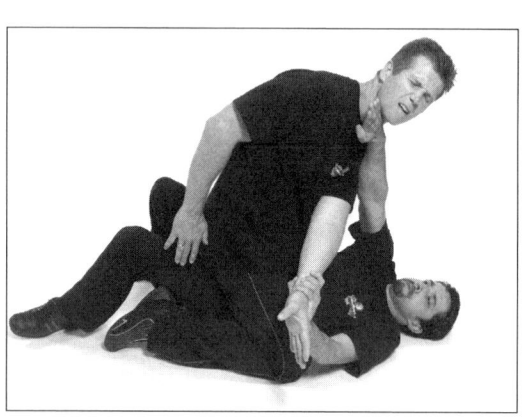
4.

Simplicity—Why Use More Movements?

Incorrect

Octavio grabs Ed's arm **(1)**. He countergrabs to control and restrain **(2)**. And continues to lock **(3)**.

1.

2.

3.

Correct

This time when Octavio grabs **(1)**, Ed just hits **(2)**.

1.

2.

Conclusion

It has been my desire to give the reader insights into the training I received from my teacher, Bruce Lee. This book constitutes just a start or the basics of Energy Training. So-called trapping hands (or legs, or body), is *not* set sequences of this to this to that. No matter how fast or impressive people may look, it is only accurate and legitimate energy application *if they are responding to their opponent's energy* or pressure. One of the benefits from training in this method is to overcome what Bruce called "flight tendency" or the feeling or need to get to a safe distance.

Once you have become comfortable in this range, you can instantaneously respond to any change your opponent makes—even the movements he does not know he is making. Part of the training involves becoming as non-telegraphic in your movements as possible. In doing so, you become much more *aware* of your opponent's slightest movements or gestures. At some point in this training, you can even sense your opponent's intentions. In one training session with Bruce I was thinking about a hit and before I could start, he shut me down and intercepted my movement with his own hit. I was merely thinking about the hit I wanted to do, so I asked: "Sifu, can you read my mind?" He just laughed and said, "I intercepted your *'intention.'*" That's when he told me that everybody telegraphs his motions. "Even I do," he admitted. But for the life of me, I could never see or feel any telegraph from him, which made me want to learn this energy training even more. Looking back, his comment triggered my commitment to "The Way."

Energy training cannot be learned in a few sessions or a weekend seminar. Mastery takes practice with a skilled teacher. The teacher, as well as the student, must possess no ego. It's the teacher's responsibility to know when ego-based attacks or one-upmanship is taking place. For example, when you get hit you try to hit right back. Doing this causes you to lose structure and sensitivity; plus, you'll usually get hit again, because your mind is focused on the wrong thing.

It will take endless hours of practice to absorb this completely. Eventually, it will become as natural as walking and talking. No conscious thought will be involved; you will seamlessly "fit in" to your opponent's every move. In contrast to kicking and hitting skills, the skills of tactile awareness improve with age and grow ever more refined. You will experience a sensation of being complete, with body and mind working in harmony. These skills do not depend on speed, power or youth; how far you take them is up to you. The potential and rewards of the energy training are limitless. It is what my teacher, Bruce Lee called, "The open end…"

About the Author

A rare and original Bruce Lee student, Jerry Poteet is known as "The Conscience of Jeet Kune Do." And no less than the editor of *Inside Kung-Fu* magazine has called him, "Unquestionably the greatest Jeet Kune Do Instructor in the world." Since his teacher's premature passing, Jerry has stood firm, refusing to water down the art that had such an enormous impact in his life. In fact, Jerry credits his teacher, Bruce Lee, with giving him the tools to survive "the fight of my life" when he was compelled to undergo a liver transplant in 1995. Today, Jerry teaches Jeet Kune Do to the next generation of students and instructors who will keep the flame alive.

Sifu Poteet has been teaching martial arts for over 40 years. Like many young men in the 1960s, Jerry began his martial arts career in Kenpo and became a black belt under renowned Kenpo grandmaster Ed Parker. But, contrary to popular misconception, Jerry did not meet his famous Jeet Kune Do teacher in Los Angeles, but in Oakland, at James Lee's house. Later that year, he was fortunate enough to be chosen as the second student admitted to Bruce Lee's Los Angeles Chinatown School. He was also selected to be in a "closed-door" group of five students who trained with Bruce Lee twice a week.

In the years since, Jerry has used his martial arts expertise to train the Dallas Cowboys football team, executive bodyguard Hollywood celebrities and handle the fight choreography of several motion pictures. But his proudest achievement came when he was chosen to train the actor who would portray his teacher, Bruce Lee, in *Dragon: The Bruce Lee Story*. Over the years, Jerry has refined a teaching method that, like the art of Jeet Kune Do itself, strips away the inessentials. He used this method to train actor Jason Scott Lee for his role as the legendary Bruce Lee. For Sifu Poteet, it was the ultimate way, "To give something back to my teacher."

Jerry truly embodies the principle of yin/yang, or opposites co-existing harmoniously. Whether teaching an individual or a group, Sifu Poteet is easy going, yet intense. He is friendly and casual in manner, yet demands precision in movement and attitude. He is all business when it comes to the training results. He wishes to illicit from students only what his teacher demanded from him—their best. It is amazing to see how many surpass not only his expectations, but theirs as well.

This is why Jerry Poteet has been proclaimed "The Source" for the truth in the art of Jeet Kune Do. For more information on Jerry Poteet's books and DVD's, call (866) 834-1249 or visit **www.up-publications.com** or **www.jerrypoteet.com**.